PLUMS OR NUTS

Bagesaanag Maagizhaa Bagaanag

Michael *Migizi* Sullivan (left) and Larry *Amik* Smallwood

PLUMS
OR
NUTS

*Bagesaanag
Maagizhaa Bagaanag*

Ojibwe Stories OF Anishinaabe Humor

Larry *Amik* Smallwood
AS TOLD TO Michael *Migizi* Sullivan Sr.

MINNESOTA
HISTORICAL
SOCIETY PRESS

Audio recordings of these stories are available on the website of the Ojibwe People's Dictionary, www.ojibwemowin.com.

mnhspress.org

The Minnesota Historical Society Press is a member of the Association of University Presses.

Manufactured in the United States of America

10 9 8 7 6 5 4 3 2

♾ The paper used in this publication meets the minimum requirements of the American National Standard for Information Sciences—Permanence for Printed Library Materials, ANSI Z39.48-1984.

International Standard Book Number
ISBN: 978-1-68134-266-5 (paper)

Library of Congress Control Number: 2023935079

CONTENTS

Locations in Minnesota and Wisconsin mentioned in the stories

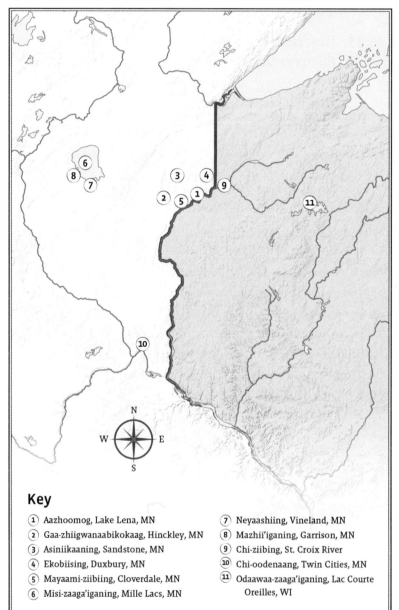

Key

1. Aazhoomog, Lake Lena, MN
2. Gaa-zhiigwanaabikokaag, Hinckley, MN
3. Asiniikaaning, Sandstone, MN
4. Ekobiising, Duxbury, MN
5. Mayaami-ziibiing, Cloverdale, MN
6. Misi-zaaga'iganing, Mille Lacs, MN
7. Neyaashiing, Vineland, MN
8. Mazhii'iganing, Garrison, MN
9. Chi-ziibing, St. Croix River
10. Chi-oodenaang, Twin Cities, MN
11. Odaawaa-zaaga'iganing, Lac Courte Oreilles, WI

PREFACE

THE STORIES CONTAINED IN THESE PAGES DO VERY LITTLE to even *begin* to scratch the surface of who Larry Amik Smallwood was—and, in many ways, still is. A father, grandfather, uncle, and namesake to many, Amik was legendary, arguably the best-known Anishinaabe of his time. He taught the Ojibwe language for almost forty years while traveling the breadth of *Anishinaabewakiing,* serving as an emcee for powwows and other Anishinaabe celebrations. There are not many Anishinaabe people that do not remember Amik. Most remark on his coolness, his signature style that was a mixture of the cowboy Indian generation he was from and a James Dean urban vibe, likely inspired by his travel in the military and considerable time spent in the Twin Cities in his early adult years. He entered the room with a confident stride and spoke in a classic baritone. He was as fond of the ladies as he was of his Marlboros, and his image is as timeless as the humor of his stories.

Amik was born on January 13, 1948, in Washington, DC, to an Anishinaabe mother and a non-Indian father. He grew up in the village of *Aazhoomog* or Lake Lena—the area that would become District III of the Mille Lacs Indian Reservation. He was raised by his mother's aunt and uncle, traditional monolingual speakers of Ojibwe, and he shares this story in *"Gii-nitaawigiyaan*/My Upbringing," in this volume. He attended an all-white school, where he quickly picked up English. He was drafted into the United States Army in 1968, and after his time in the service, he moved to Los Angeles, California, through the US government's urban Indian relocation program. In 1971 he returned to Minnesota, where he began his illustrious career as an educator of the Anishinaabe language and culture.

Amik was proud of his children, but he rarely took anything else very seriously. Pretty much everything was a target for his jokes. It was only while spending time with him, especially in the winter months, that I grew to know about his passion for our wintertime *aadizookaan*. A phenomenal storyteller, Amik took us back to a different time with his stories and shared parts of our language and our worldview that just do not transfer well into print. In many ways, the stories and travels of Amik's life show great parallels to Wenabozho himself, and many of us have noticed those striking similarities.

Amik lived his life close to *gimishoomisinaanig naa gookomisinaan,* the ceremonial drums of the Mille Lacs Band. He was a member of many drums, frequently called upon to speak for drum ceremonies and help with the music. He shares here in this collection how he was traumatized as a youth and returned to a traditional Anishinaabe spiritual path later in life. He was proud of our way of life, proud of his people, and hopeful regarding the future of the Ojibwe language.

I first met Amik when I was about twelve years old. He was working at the school in Lac Courte Oreilles (LCO) with the elders and language teaching staff and was a regular emcee at our powwows. He took a liking to me then, as I was interested in powwow singing and Ojibwe language. We were of the same clan, and he reminded me of that regularly. We grew to become friends, and he mentored me in the powwow arena, as both a singer at the drum and a budding emcee on the microphone. As I dove deeper into my language learning and linguistic research, he quickly became my most trusted linguistic consultant, teacher, and model for language production.

While he had a reputation of being critical and rather intimidating to young learners of Ojibwe, he was both gracious and patient with me, always insisting that I speak like him, regardless of whoever else taught me. If there was one thing that he wanted us to learn as new speakers of Ojibwe, it was the humor. He was a master of Anishinaabe shock humor, saying things that were drastically inappropriate by mainstream standards—but he and many others insisted on the teaching of *our* humor and *our* standards! As can be seen in the stories that follow, nothing was off-limits for a good joke.

When I first went to record Amik, he was working at the Mille Lacs Band's Immersion Grounds in Rutledge, Minnesota. I drove over from LCO and arrived early in the morning. When I showed up at his office, he offered me coffee and then asked me if I knew how to change a tire. When I told him yes, I know how to change a tire, he asked, "Yeah, but can you change a tire in Ojibwe?" He wanted us to know practical language. He had me turn on the recorder, and then he told me a story about going to Minneapolis and getting a flat on the freeway. Step by step, he walked through the process of changing the tire in Ojibwe, exemplifying the classic storytelling conventions and event sequencing signature of a distinguished

Ojibwe storyteller. He told me to type it up and translate it and bring it back if I wanted to do more. This must have been his way of testing me. I was at his office the next morning, even before he arrived, with the story typed up and translated—and my recorder, ready for more. That first story, "*Gii-paashkijiisijigeyaan*/When I Had a Blowout," appears in this volume.

That story led to many others. We recorded often at his office in Rutledge, or in Minneapolis where I was a graduate student. Sometimes we worked at his house in Hinckley, and a few times he came to LCO to meet me. We recorded a few short stories each time, and sometimes he had a song he wanted me to record, or a funny expression or saying that he wanted to be documented. After each session, I transcribed the stories, calling him frequently for clarification on words or form or issues that arose regarding translation. When going to see him again, I printed copies of the latest draft stories for his review, and each time he would reply, "When is the book coming out?" Not so much concerned with quality control, he was eager to get his stories into the hands of the many students he had taught over the years.

To know Amik was to know his humor and to wonder about the lore that surrounded him. The reader now can seek the truth in his stories as well as the fabrication. We revel in his tales of Gizhaagamide, his uncle Netaawaash, who is affectionately known here as "Hot Water." He also shares stories of his peers Junior and Obizaan, immersed right beside him in the language and culture of the Anishinaabe. His mentions of alcohol are numerous, revealing what a turbulent time his generation had in growing up.

Since Amik was so linguistically influential in the Southwestern (SW) Ojibwe region, I offer some information here regarding his variety of Ojibwe and some of his preferences for how his language is represented in print. First and foremost is the use of the Fiero or Double Vowel writing system, which inadvertently standardized the spelling of Ojibwe in this area. Amik was a staunch opponent of it, preferring to spell Ojibwe phonetically (really, however it sounded to him). Amik long rejected working with anyone who would spell his words in a manner different from how he prescribed. That is, until I had the opportunity to convince him.

After attending a community class he was teaching in Minneapolis, I noticed he had spelled the phrase *mii iw,* roughly *that's it,* three different ways (*me iw, mii ew,* and *me iwe*). I asked him to pronounce each one for me, and each was the same. I pointed out that although his system worked wonderfully for him, he might think about how his students would be able to make sense out of the same phrase being spelled three different ways. I then explained the only significant difference between his way and the Double Vowel system was the representation of the vowel sounds. Given this opportunity to see why the Double Vowel system was winning out among second-language learners, he was able to let up and began using the writing system himself. "I threw in the towel," *gii-ikido.*

Much of the vocabulary here is presented as Amik said it, or as he preferred it written. Verbs like *bishaga'aakwe vai* (s/he peels logs) or *baataniinowag vai* (they are plentiful; numerous) as well as adverbs like *apaapii* (every once in a while) and sometimes *genapii* (eventually) represent personal preferences and distinctions from the perhaps more standard *bishagaakwe, baatayiinowag, ayaapii,* and *gegapii.* Other variations include *abinoojiins,* though on other occasions I had manage to elicit *abinoo-jiinyens* from him with no objection. Frequent in traditional Anishinaabe stories, the phrase *aaniish-naa* is represented here as such, in accordance with Amik's preference, although varying pronunciations attested in the recordings include *nish-naa, anish-naa, aniish-naa.*

Because Amik was strongly biliterate, he had opinions regarding how his words were represented in print. Anyone who had the opportunity to hear Amik speak remembers him saying, *"kina gegoo"* or *"Mii keyaa!"* When presenting such phrases in the transcriptions, Amik had a strong preference for restorations of the initial /a/, as in **a**kina and **a**keyaa, but not the initial /g/ common in the speech of other elders in his community, **g**akina, **g**akeyaa. Similarly, phrases like *booch dash kawe* are represented here as *booch dash* **a**kawe. Amik was well aware of "proper speech" as well as his slang and made the choice to restore the vowels. Similarly, he went back and forth with *zhigwa* and **a**zhigwa, with no apparent difference in usage or preference. I have done my best to write each as he pronounced them.

His classic Mille Lacs speech, with the more eastern variety of *Aazhoomog*, is represented well here. Amik rarely used *ji-*, the infinitival tense marker with the feeling of *to; in order to; for the purpose of,* replacing it almost completely with *da-*, a prominent feature of the Wisconsin varieties. Similarly, *jibwaa-*, the standard in SW Ojibwe for *before,* was usually *dabwaa-* for Amik and others from *Aazhoomog*. Although I do have a few cases of *ji-* and *jibwaa-* appearing in my work with Amik, neither appears here in these stories. Language learners will also notice what they may consider irregularities concerning dependent animate noun stems such as *ogookomisan* (h/ grandmother) differing from the prescribed, perhaps more standard *ookomisan*. Such is the case for other dependent noun stems in the pages that follow, including *wiitaan* (h/ brother-in-law, said by a male), with varying *owiitaawaan/wiitaawaan* for "their brother(s)-in-law" (3p>3'). Of course, we must not forget his intentional and purposeful habit of incorporating English in his Ojibwe storytelling, which always seems to add yet another layer of humor—for example, **ogramaamaay-ibaniin** (h/ late gramma).

Amik was an exemplary speaker of *Ojibwemowin*, or Southwestern (SW) Ojibwe, and was considered an authority on the language in the SW region. He encouraged second-language learners to "Make sure you sound like you're *from* somewhere!" suggesting that you can tell where someone is from based on how they speak. He was, without question, an *Aazhoomog* speaker, and he was proud of the features that defined that. He had a knack for using participles, a main variable in Ojibwe dialectology, and he was aware of the regional parameters, taking great pride in his southern *Ojibwemowin*. Many of the mysteries I had as a researcher and language learner that surround the verbal endings like *-jig*, *-nijin*, *-igojin*, *-aajin*, and others were solved with Amik as my main linguistic consultant.

Language learners grappling with mastering the infamous VTA (transitive animate verb) paradigm are often shocked to discover that Amik preferred the pattern *ni-verb-in* for the "I verb you" conjugation, which from an English perspective is more intuitive than the standard *gi-verb-in* pattern prescribed by most first-language speakers and language teachers. When calling attention to it, he always said, "I know everyone says *Giwiidookoon*, but *Niwiidookoon* makes sense to me"—almost as if his certain speech peculiarities were conscious decisions he made. When teaching his students the common departing salutation, *giga-waabamin* (I'll see you), Amik often taught *ga-waabamin*, the colloquial, cool way of saying it, omitting the personal prefix altogether. In the story "*Aamoog*/The Bees," he mentions *giziindime'igan*, his preferred way of saying "toilet paper," over *giziindime'on*, the more standard word, because according to Amik, *giziindime'on* (vai singular imperative) sounds like, "Wipe your ass!"

The English versions of Amik's stories are generally free, running translations that usually were proposed by me, then modified or approved by Amik. Amik wanted the English pages to reflect the way he spoke English; he wanted them to sound like him. This led to complications in translation, since we were also trying to capture the meaning of the Ojibwe. One such example is with the word *geget*, which means *sure, certainly, really, indeed*. In the book's title story, "*Bagesaanag Maagizhaa Bagaanag*/Plums or Nuts," Amik beings by saying, "*Geget zanagad maajaa'iweng*." When I proposed the translation, "Indeed, conducting funerals is difficult," Amik scoffed, "Indeed? I don't say *indeed*." After considering other translations, such as "Surely, conducting funerals is difficult," and "Conducting funerals is truly difficult," Amik settled on, "Indeed, doing funerals is hard."

Advanced language learners know that all of the above translations are possible and perhaps equally acceptable, but the translation that appears here is Amik's approved version—even though he didn't really ever say "indeed."

Other notable issues with translation involve the English word used for *Anishinaabe, Anishinaabeg,* etc. Dictionary entries list "a person, a human, an Indian, an Ojibwe"; Amik preferred the colloquial Ojibberlish (Ojibwe + English) translation, *Shinaab(s).* As a result, the translation of *Anishinaabe(g)* is often *Shinaab(s).* Certain exclamatory expressions such as *wayaa* or *wa!* (short for *howa!*) are often not translated at all, as Amik preferred to use them in his translation, rather than forcing them into an English characterization that didn't sound right to him. A number of other common Ojibwe words appear in the English text, again reflecting Amik's spoken English; readers can find them in the glossary. Certain frequent Ojibwe words such as *imaa, omaa, a'aw,* and *iniw* often aren't included at all in the translations, as adding a *there, here, that,* or *those* made the translation more awkward. Other terms used in translation, such as *popples,* represent preferences for reservation vernacular over more standard English terms like *poplar.*

Although I have striven to represent Amik's stories as accurately as possible, I have made certain revisions to the Ojibwe, as well as to the English. Cases of false starts and certain cases of repetition have been omitted from print. Readers interested in knowing how the text differs from the audio recordings should consult the textual notes that follow the stories. All are encouraged to listen to the stories and hear Amik bring these tales to life. The recordings are housed online on the website of The Ojibwe People's Dictionary, ojibwemowin.com. Any mistakes that occur in the Ojibwe or the English are all mine.

Amik began his journey on April 11, 2017, much sooner than many of us close to him had expected. His youthful nature and active lifestyle had us convinced that we would have at least another ten years with him. While many in other cultures or traditions might give up with the passing of such a significant cultural figure, Amik's passing lit a spark for many in the Anishinaabe community and refueled the fires of others already engaged. His students have stepped up—many have been called upon to fill the numerous vacancies he left in the ceremonial drum societies, and many are serving as officiants for funerals, naming ceremonies, first-kill feasts, and other important traditional ceremonies that rely on the Ojibwe language. Several of Amik's students are now language instructors, from university faculty to immersion-school teachers. His words live on in the effort to reclaim the Ojibwe language.

As the editor of this volume and the individual to whom he told his stories, I had every intention to get this book published while Amik was still with us. His unexpected passing was hard for many of us. Though I tried right away to proofread these pages and check my transcriptions against the recordings, it was just too difficult to do this so soon after his passing. Hearing his voice and reading his words was hard. I put it all away and committed to seeing the project through when the time was right. As some years have gone by and we remember him with smiles instead of sadness, the time is now. Many people will be delighted with its long-overdue publication. I hope the stories are as enjoyable to the readers as they were for us.

As I review the contents of this collection one more time, I can see how Amik continues to inspire us to do more for our people. Each story reminds me of the recording sessions—and reminds me of other stories, stories that came about by our friendship. I am inspired by the fascinating life of Amik, a cultural icon of the Ojibwe who, like other historical icons in our culture, lives on forever through our stories. *Miigwech Amikogaabaw weweni gikinoo'amawiyaang. Gaawiin wiikaa giga-wanenimigoosiin.*

Michael *Migizi* Sullivan Sr., PhD
1zd Onaabani-giizis 2023
Odaawaa-zaaga'iganing

PLUMS OR NUTS

Bagesaanag Maagizhaa Bagaanag

Gii-nitaawigiyaan

[1] MII DASH IWIDI GII-PABAA-AYAAWAAD INGOJI A'AW
nimaamaayiban miinawaa indedeyiban. Gegoo ko gii-
izhichige aw indedeyiban. Ogii-kimoodinan zhooniyaan
imaa zhooniyaawigamigong mii gaa-izhichiged
baashkizigan ko ogii-aabajitoon.

[2] Mii dash iwidi *Maryland* besho go imaa
Waashtanong ezhinikaadeg *Washington D.C.*, mii imaa
gii-ayaawaad imaa ingoji. Mii dash imaa ingoding
bimi-ayaawaad ingiw dakoniwewininiwag ogii-
nisidawinawaawaan iniw indedeyibaniin. Miish imaa
gaa-izhi-ganawaabamaawaad, namanj minik. Miish gaa-
izhi-ganoonaawaad aanind bakaan dakoniwewininiwag
gii-pi-izhaawaad ogii-pi-gibishkaagowaan imaa.

[3] Mii dash imaa gii-kashkaabika'igaazod a'aw
indedeyiban mii maajiinind. Gii-nandabijigaazowan
iniw odoodaabaanan mii imaa gii-mikigaadeg iniw
baashkiziganan miinawaa imaa gii-mikigaazowan
zhooniyaansan gaa-michi-ozhi'aajin gaye.

[4] Mii dash gaye niin nimaamaayiban gaa-izhi-
mamigaazod. Ingii-ningodwaaso-giiziswagiz. Mii
iwidi nimaamaa gewiin gaa-izhiwinind endazhi-
ganawenimindwaa ingiw ikwewag. Miish aw
indedeyiban gaa-izhi-gibaakwa'ond, gii-aapidaakwa'waa
dash.

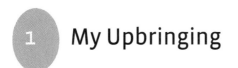

1   My Upbringing

[1] MY MOTHER AND FATHER USED TO TRAVEL ALL AROUND. There is something my father used to do. He stole money from banks, that's what he did, using a gun when he did it.

[2] It was over in Maryland, near the place called *Waashtanong,* Washington, DC, they were somewhere around there. Then this one time the police came along, and they recognized my dad. They were watching him for a while, I don't know how long. So those cops called for backup, and when backup arrived, they blocked him in.

[3] And then my dad was handcuffed and taken away. They searched his car and that is where they found his guns and they found the [counterfeit] money that he had made too.

[4] Then they took me and my mom too. I was six months old. So, they took my mom to the women's shelter. Then my father was locked up, for good.

[5] Mii dash omaa ongow gaa-nitaawigi'ijig omaa
Aazhoomog gii-piijibii'amawindwaa minjiminigaazod
nimaamaa miinawaa gaye niin imaa gii-wiij'ayaawag.
Gaa-izhi-anoonaawaad iniw nizhishenyibaniin
a'aw Naawigiizis gaa-izhinikaazod *James Clark*. Gaa-
izhi-anoonaawaad, "Indaga o-nandawaabam a'aw
abinoojiins iwidi Waashtanong gidaa-bi-azhewinaa
omaa. Mii omaa da-ganawenimangid."

[6] Gaa-izhi-nakodang a'aw Naawigiizisoban. Gaa-
izhi-boozid imaa Asiniikaaning, *Sandstone* iniw
ishkodewidaabaanan. Gii-maajaad iwidi akeyaa
Waashtanong gii-izhaad. Namanj minik gaa-
tazhitaagwen aw ishkodewidaabaan gii-tagoshing
iwidi maagizhaa nisogon, niiwogon.

[7] Mii dash iwidi gii-paa-nandawaabamid gii-paa-
nandawaabamaad ge iniw nimaamaayan aandi
endazhi-minjiminimind. Mii gii-paa-nandawaabamaad
nimaamaayibaniin aandi gaa-tazhi-minjiminigaazonid.
Miish gii-mikawaad, shke wiindamawaad,
"Niwii-azhegiiwewinaa wa'aw abinoojiinh iwidi
da-wiij'ayaawaad iniw chi-aya'aan iwidi Aazhoomog."

[8] Miish gaa-izhi-bagidinigooyaan gaa-izhi-bagidinind
sa go da-bi-azhegiiwewizhid. Mii miinawaa
ishkodewidaabaaning gii-poozid miinawaa gii-pi-
izhiwizhid omaa Asiniikaaning imaa gii-kabaad miish
miinawaa imaa gii-izhiwizhid idi Aazhoomog gii-
pagamiwizhid.

[5] So then, those ones that raised me in *Aazhoomog* were informed by letter of where my mother was being held and that I was with her, too. So, they hired my uncle *Naawigiizis,* the one named James Clark. So, they hired him, "Please go look for that baby in Washington and bring him back here. We'll take care of him here."

[6] So *Naawigiizis* agreed. He then boarded the train in Sandstone. He headed out for Washington. I don't know how long it took him for the train to arrive, three maybe four days.

[7] Then he went around looking all over for me there, and he looked for where my mother was being held too, where she was being cared for. Then when he found her, he told her, "I'm going to take him home to stay with those elders in *Aazhoomog.*"

[8] So they released me, or rather they allowed him to bring me back. Then he got back on the train and brought me back here. He got off and took me to *Aazhoomog* and delivered me there.

[9] Mii imaa gaa-onji-maajii-nitaawigiyaan, mii
gaa-onji-maajii-nitaawigi'iwaad ingiw chi-aya'aag.
Nashke, gaawiin aapiji gii-shaaganaashiimosiiwag
gaye. Mii dash iwidi gaa-izhi-izhaawaad iwidi *Pine
City* gii-o-mooshkinebii'amowaad mazina'iganan
da-bagidinindwaa da-ganawenimiwaad
da-bagidinindwaa da-ganawenimigooyaan. Mii dash
imaa gaa-onji-nitaawigiyaan ingiw chi-aya'aag gii-
pami'iwaad.

[10] Nashke, ingoding igo gaa-ningo-biboonagak mii iw
gii-pagidinind aw nimaamaayiban da-bi-azhegiiwed.
Aaniish-naa wiin gaawiin gegoo gii-izhichigesiin mii
aw indedeyiban gaa-kagiibaadizid akina gegoo gaa-
izhichiged. Miish gaa-izhi-aapidaakwa'ond, nashke, gaa
wiikaa ingii-waabamaasiin a'aw.

[11] Mii dash gaa-pi-dagoshing nimaamaayiban omaa
gii-pi-wiij'ayaawaad iniw chi-aya'aan ajina. Gaa-izhi-
wiindamawaawaad, "Daga neyaab o-baa-nandawanokiin
ingoji bakaan, maagizhaa giga-mikwanokii
iwidi miinawaa chi-oodenaang izhaayan. Gego
babaamenimaaken a'aw gwiiwizens niinawind omaa
inga-bami'aanaan. Miinawaa ge iishpin awiya mikawad
ge-wiij'ayaawad miinawaa, mii iw miinawaa ge-izhi-
maajitaayamban miinawaa," gii-inaa.

[12] Miish geget iwidi chi-oodenaang miinawaa gii-
paa-nandawanokiid. Gii-mikwanokii iwidi miinawaa
endazhi-ozhichigaadenig wiiwakwaanan, mii iwidi
akeyaa gii-anokiid.

[9] So that's how my upbringing began, that is how those elders began to raise me. You see, they didn't speak very much English either. So, then they went over to Pine City and filled out the papers to make it legal to take care of me, for them to take care of me. That there is how I grew up with those elders having adopted me.

[10] You see, sometime a year later my mother was allowed to come back. After all, she didn't do anything; it was my father that was the foolish one that did everything. So, they locked him up forever, you see, I never saw him.

[11] Then after my mom arrived here, she stayed with those elders for a little while. Then they told her, "Just go back and look for work somewhere else, maybe you'll find work in the big city if you go there. Don't worry about this little boy; we will raise him. And maybe you'll find someone you will want to be with, and you can start over again," she was told.

[12] So sure enough, she went to the big city again to look for work. She found work over there again in a hat-making factory; that is what she did for work.

[13] Ingii-izhaa, nigezikwendaan gii-izhaayaambaan iwidi aabiding endazhi-anokiid a'aw nimaamaayiban maagizhaa gaa-niso-biboonagiziwaanen. Aaniish mii iw, mii iwidi gii-waabamangid mii iwidi megwaa anokiid. Mii miinawaa idi gii-mikawaad iniw ininiwan gii-wiidigemaad, gaa-mino-doodaagojin.

[14] Indayaawaag dash nishiimeyag, nishiimeyag indayaawaag. Mii iw dash imaa bizaan gii-ayayaayaan gii-pami'iwaad ingiw chi-aya'aag. Ingoding maagizhaa go ingoji maagizhaa gaa-niizhwaaso-biboonagiziwaanen, gaawiin, maagizhaa ningodwaaso-biboonagiziwaanen gii-pi-bagamibizod imaa aw odaabaan aabiding. Chi-mookomaanikwe imaa gabaa odakonaanan mazina'iganan mii iw biindiged imaa gaa-taayaang. Miish aw mindimooyenyiban nimaamaans sa go ingii-izhi-wiinaa, aw gaa-nitaawigi'id, "Daga naazh a'aw mindimooyenh idi besho eyaad da-bi-aanikanootamawid." "Ahaw." Mii imaa gii-mooshkinebii'amowaagwen ini mazina'iganan, giiwenh da-gikinoo'amaagoziyaan azhigwa.

[15] Mii dash imaa netamising gii-piinjwebinigooyaan *1st grade*. Gaawiin ge ingii-nitaa-zhaaganaashiimosiin. Miinawaa ge gaawiin besho imaa ingii-ayaasiimin ishkoniganing. Bakaan imaa awas bangii ingii-taamin. Nashke wiin idi aanind ingiw Anishinaabensag Anishinaabe-gikinoo'amaadiiwigamigong gii-izhaawag iwidi, niin dash mii eta go bizhishig Chi-mookomaanag imaa gaa-ayaajig.

[13] I went there, I can remember going there once where my mother worked; maybe I was about three years old. We saw her there while she was working. It is there that she found another man and married him, one that treated her good.

[14] I have younger siblings. I stayed content being adopted by those elders. Sometime when I was around seven years old, a car pulled in one day. A white lady got out holding papers and went into our house. That old lady, well I called her my mom, that one who raised me, "Go get that old lady that lives close by to come translate for me." "Okay." There they must have filled out those papers, supposedly it was time for me to go to school.

[15] They threw me into first grade. I wasn't very fluent in English, either. We also didn't live very close to the reservation. We lived just a little way off. See, some of those other Anishinaabe children went to an Indian school, but as for me, I went to an all-white school.

[16] Gaawiin ge ingii-nitaa-agindaasosiin gaawiin ge ingii-nitaa-zhaaganaashiimosiin. Ingoji go *September,* mii dash azhigwa gaa-waawaabandamaan akina gegoo imaa gaa-ozhibii'igaadegin imaa ishpiming, ezhinikaadamowaad *alphabet,* gaganawaabandamaan iko miinawaa iniw mazina'igaansan gaa-agindamowaajin mii ge imaa gii-waabandamaan iniw. Mii dash imaa gii-ni-maajii-nitaa-zhaaganaashiimoyaan bangii.

[17] Ingoji go ningo-giizis ingii-gikinoo'amaagoz apii imaa gii-ikidoyaan *my first English sentence.* Gii-mazinaakizo imaa ikwezens izhinoo'waad iniw gaazhagensan bimibatoonid. Niibawiwan dash imaa ganabaj omaamaayan mazinaakizon mazinaakizonid. Mii gaa-izhising iw, "See the cat run." Wa. Niganawaabandaan iw miinawaa iniw ozhibii'igaansan imaa gaa-agoodegin niwaabandaan miinawaa iw mazina'igan gaa-agindamaang. Mii iidog giiwenh aaniish-naa, bimibatoo gaazhagenzhish, mii iidog ekidogwen aw, "See the cat run," Wa! "Ganabaj naa nizhaaganaashiim," indinendam.

[18] Mii eta go gaa-mikwendamaan gabe-giizhik. Mii dash gaa-ani-dagoshinaan ishkwaa-gikinoo'amaading ani-dagoshinaan iwidi endaayaang, "Maam, daga omaa bi-izhaan." Gaa-izhi-debibinag aw gaazhagenzhish. "Omaa agwajiing bi-izhaan." "Aaniin da?" ikido. "Ke inga-waabanda'in gegoo." Gaa-izhi-bagidinag a'aw gaazhagenzhish, hay' mii gaawiin gii-maajiibatoosiin. Gaa-izhi-chi-basikawaanag aw gaa-ani-maajiibatood miinawaa, "See the cat run," indinaa mindimooyenh. Mii eta go chi-ganawaabamid.

[16] I couldn't read very well, and I couldn't speak very good English. Sometime in September, that is when I observed the things that were written above, what they call the alphabet, I looked through those little books that they read and saw those. That's where I started to become good at speaking English a little bit.

[17] About a month into school is when I said my first English sentence. There was a picture of a girl pointing at a cat running. I think it might have been her mother standing there in the picture. And what it said was, "See the cat run." *Wa.* I looked at the alphabet hanging there and then I looked down at the words that I read. That must be it; after all, the cat is running. That must be what they are saying, "See the cat run." *Wa.* "I think I'm speaking English," I thought.

[18] That's all I remembered all day long. After I got home after school, "Mom, could you please come here." So, then I grabbed the cat. "Come outside." "What the—?" she said. "Check this out, I'm going to show you something." So, I put the cat down and he didn't even run. So, I kicked it really good and it took off running, "See the cat run," I said to that old lady. All she did was look at me just hard.

[19] Gaa-izhi-naanag miinawaa aw gaazhagenzhish,
"Shke omaa inga-zhaaganaashiim miinawaa."
Bagidinag aw gaazhagens dabwaa-basikawaanag gaa-
izhi-maajiibatood, *See the cat run,* indinaa. "Aaniin
danaa? Daga naa booni' aw gaazhagenzhish. Aaniin
ezhiwebiziyan?"

[20] Mii imaa *my first English sentence.* Mii iw gaa-
onji-gikinoo'amaagoziyaan, mii dash ingoji *in December*
mii iw apii gii-nitaa-zhaaganaashiimoyaan. Gaawiin
ge wiikaa ingii-wanendanziin iw Ojibwemowin. Mii
dash ow gii-nitaa-zhaaganaashiimoyaan akina gegoo.
Gaawiin ge wiikaa ingii-minjiminigoosiin ingii-
ishkonigoosiin imaa da-mamooyaan miinawaa iw;
I never flunked a grade.

[21] Ingoji dash, ganabaj *in the fifth grade* ingii-
ayaamin eko-naaning ingii-waabamaa imaa
aabiding bi-bagamibizod agwajiing odaabaan
gikinoo'amaagoziyaang, "Awenesh waa-izhaad iwidi
Religious Instructions?" ikido gikinoo'amaagekwe.
Aa, zhiibinikeniwag ingiw Chi-mookomaanensag,
gaa-izhi-gagwejimag a'aw waadabimag, "Awegonesh
ge iw *Religious Instructions?*" "Oonh, mii iwidi
ganawaabandang mezinaateseg bebakaan awiya chi-
agaaming endaajig akina gegoo inga-waabanda'igoomin
imaa mazinaateseg." Aaniish-naa gaawiin ingii-
ayaanziimin iw mazinaatesijigan. "Miinawaa ge
menwaagamig gimina'igoomin bakwezhigaansag
ge ga-ashamigoo." "Wa, mii gaye niin azhigwa wii-
izhaayaan imaa *Religious Instructions.*"

[19] So I went after the cat again, "See I'm going to speak English again." When I put the cat down and before I kicked it, it took off running. "See the cat run," I said to her. "What the heck? Leave that ol' cat alone. What is the matter with you?"

[20] That there was my first English sentence. That is how I learned, and then sometime around December is when I spoke pretty good English. I never did forget the Ojibwe language either. This is how I became fluent in English. Also, I was never held back a grade or anything; I never flunked a grade.

[21] I think it was around the time when we were in the fifth grade, I saw a car pull up one time when we were in school, "Who wants to go to religious instructions?" said the female teacher. Oh, those little white kids raised their arms, and I asked the one who I was sitting with, "What are religious instructions?" "Oh, we watch movies about different people from across the ocean. They show us everything in those movies." Well, of course we didn't have TVs. "They give us Kool-Aid to drink, they feed you cookies." "*Wa,* now I want to go to religious instructions too!"

[22] Namanj daching endaso-anama'e-giizhik gii-pi-izhaa aw akiwenzhiiyish. Ingoding gaa-izhi-wiindamaaged imaa, "Iishpin bizaan-ayaasiweg, iishpin bangii giiwanimoyeg, iishpin igo bangii giimoojichigeyeg gegoo, mii akina awiya mii da-jaagizoyeg. A'aw Gizhe-manidoo owii-chaagizaan ow aki." Oonh yay, niwaanda-biingeyendam naa wenji-ikidod iw.

[23] Mii miinawaa gaa-izhi-izhaayaan idi ishkwaa-gikinoo'amaading gaa-izhi-giiweyaan miinawaa mii miinawaa gii-wiindamawag aw mindimooyenyiban, "Gigikendaan ina ingoding giwii-chaagizomin akina?" "Aaniin danaa ekidoyan?" "Geget giwii-chaagizomin akina, mii iw gaa-ikidod a'aw Chi-mookomaan noongom mekadekonayed." "Gego ganage debwetawaaken a'aw, gego miinawaa gaye izhaaken imaa. Gaawiin gidaa-doodaagosiinaan giinawind gimanidoominaan, gizhawenimigonaan. Bakaan wiin ingiw Chi-mookomaanag odizhi-debweyendaanaawaa gegoo. Mii wenji-bagidinang giinawind aw asemaa wenji-biindaakoonang aw manidoo da-ganawenimigooyang. Gizhawenimigonaan, gego debwetawaaken igo."

[24] Mii dash imaa gii-maajii-zegiziyaan imaa. Ingii-piindaakoojige ko, miinawaa ingii-kiimoodanami'aa. Ingii-kanoonaa ko gewiin aw *Jesus* ezhinikaazod. Ginwenzh ingii-izhichige iw. Baamaa dash igo ganabaj ingii-nisimidana-ashi-niizhobiboonagiz, mii gii-maaminonendamaan, bezhigo aw manidoo naagaanizid.

[22] I don't know how many weeks that old man came over. One time, he tells everyone, "If you all aren't well behaved, even if you tell a little lie, if you do bad in a sneaky way, every one of you will burn. Jesus is going to burn up the Earth." Oh no, I was just bewildered by why he would say that.

[23] So then again when I went home after school, I told that old lady, "Do you know that one day we are all going to burn?" "Why the heck are you saying that?" "Yup, we're all going to burn, that is what that white preacher said today." "Don't you even believe him and don't go back there! Our creator wouldn't do that to us, he loves us. The *Chi-mookomaan* believes in a different way. That is why we put tobacco down, why we offer it to the Creator, so we are taken care of. He loves us. Don't believe him!"

[24] So that is where I started getting scared. I would put tobacco out and I would sneak-pray too. I prayed to the one they call Jesus too. For a long time I did this. It was not until, I think I was about thirty-two years old, that is when I realized that there is only one Creator.

[25] Bebakaan gigii-izhi-miinigoomin, bebakaan gigii-izhi-miinigoomin da-izhitwaayang. Mii ge bebakaan gigii-izhi-miinigoomin da-inweyang. Mii dash imaa gii-moonendamaan iw, "Oonh indanishinaabew. Asemaa inga-aabaji'aa, indinwewin inga-aabajitoon ganoonag aw manidoo. Gaawiin miinawaa wiikaa indaa-ganoonaasiin aw *Jesus*. Chi-mookomaan ingwana wiin a'aw." Mii imaa gii-kwayakoseyaan dash dibishkoo go ingii-mikodaadiz. Mii akeyaa gaa-izhi-nitaawigiyaan.

[25] We were given different things, different ways to practice our spiritualities. And we were given different languages. It is then that I realized, "Oh, I am Anishinaabe. I will use my tobacco and I will use my language when I talk to the *manidoo*. Never again will I talk to Jesus. Here it turns out that is the *Chi-mookomaan*'s way." From then on, I straightened out just like I had found my identity. That is how I grew up.

2 Aaniin Bagonez!

[1] ANOOJ KO OGII-INAAWAAN INIW CHI-MOOKOMAANAN ingiw Anishinaabeg mewinzha. Shke imaa gii-ayaa imaa adaawewinini imaa Aazhoomog besho. Aaniish-naa, mii imaa gaa-ondinigewaad ingiw Anishinaabeg.

[2] Anooj ko gii-ikido aw Chi-mookomaanish, apane gagwejimaad gegoo Anishinaaben gegoo. Mii nitam gaa-gikendang, *"How do you say, hi- hello?"* "Oo, Aaniin." Mii gaa-izhi-gikendang, "Aaniin."

[3] Awiya biindigenid, "Aaniin!" Aabiding gaa-izhi-gagwedwed imaa, "Aaniin ekidong awiya, *"How do you say, 'Hello friend, my good friend?'"* Awegwesh gaa-wiindamawaagwen, anooj ogii-toodawaawaan, mii gaa-izhi-wiindamawaawaad ingiw ininiwag, "Oo, bagonez. 'Aaniin bagonez!', mii ge-ikidoyamban," ogii-inaawaan iniw Chi-mookomaanishan. "Miish iw geget."

[4] Aah, awiya biindigenid imaa, "Aaniin bagonez!" Wa. Chi-ganawaabamigod iniw ko iniw Anishinaaben apane gaa-ikidod. Aabiding dash gaa-izhi-wiindamawind, awiya gaa-izhi-wiindamaagod iniw ikwewan, "Gego inaaken awiya iw 'bagonez'." "Aaniin dash?" "Gimaji-izhinikaanaa. *That means 'you with the hole'.*"

2 Hey, You with the Hole!

[1] THE ANISHINAABE PEOPLE USED TO SAY ALL KINDS OF
things to the *Chi-mookomaan* a long time ago. See, there
was a storekeeper over near *Aazhoomog*. Well, that's
where the Anishinaabe people got their stuff.

[2] That ol' white guy would say all kinds of things,
always asking the Shinaabs about something. This is
the first thing that he knew, "How do you say 'hi—
hello'?" "Ooh, *Aaniin*." So then he knew, "*Aaniin*."

[3] When someone came in, "*Aaniin!*" Then one time
he asked, "How does one say, 'Hello my good friend'?" I
don't know who it was that told him, they did all kinds
of things to him, then the men told him, "Oh, '*Bagonez*.
Aaniin bagonez,' that is what you should say," they told
that ol' white guy. "That's it!"

[4] Then when someone came in, "*Aaniin bagonez!*"
Wa. Those Shinaabs would just look really hard at him
when he would always say that. But then one time he
was told, it was a woman who had told him, "Don't
say '*bagonez*' to anyone." "How come?" "You are calling
them by a bad name. That means 'you with the hole.'"

[5] Wa, chi-baapid a'aw Chi-mookomaanish, aaniish-
naa gii-kagiibaadizi, miish geget igo miish geget awiya
biindigenid imaa mii go booch igo, "Aaniin bagonez!"
Aaniin bagonez!

[5] *Wa,* that ol' white guy laughed really hard, after all, he was foolish, so of course when someone would come in there, he just had to say, *"Aaniin bagonez!"* Hey, you with the hole!

3 Akakojiish

[1] AABIDING GE INGOJI INGII-ASHI-BEZHIGO-BIBOONAGIZ ganabaj maagizhaa ashi-niizho-biboonagiziyaan, gaa-izhi-mamooyaan iw baashkizigaans iw niishtana ashi-niizh enigokwaag, megwayaak baa-ayaayaan imaa, ziigwang.

[2] Gaa-izhi-waabamag aw akakojiish. Imbaa-wiijiiwaa indayish. Wayaa, gaa-izhi-baashkizwag gaa-izhi-bishkonawag. Miish imaa chi-mitig imaa badakizod mii imaa biinjayi'ii imaa, wiimbizinid mii imaa gii-piindigeyooded aw akakojiish.

[3] Ninoondawaa igo omaa ingoji go besho go omaa biinjayi'ii imaa mitigong niikimod a'aw akakojiish. Aaniish-naa gii-shegoode imaa. Miish imaa indayish endazhi-migid. "Ahaw, gii-shegoode ganabaj inga-biinjiniken imaa inga-debibidoowaan iw ozow. Inga-chi-wiikoobinaa dash imaa miish imaa inday da-giikamaad," indinendam.

[4] Gaa-izhi-biinjinikeniyaan imaa wii-nandoojiinamaan iw ozow, gaa-izhi-gichi-dakwamid a'aw akakojiish. Wayaa, gaa-chi-wiisagendamaan, chi-biibaagiyaan imaa, oonh yay giiwebatooyaan imaa.

3 The Woodchuck

[1] ONE TIME I WAS ELEVEN YEARS OLD, OR MAYBE WHEN I was twelve years old, I took a gun, a 22-caliber rifle, with me as I went around out there in the woods, in the springtime.

[2] Then I saw a woodchuck. I have my dog along with me. *Wayaa,* so I shot, missing him. There's a big tree standing there and inside of it, in the hollow, that woodchuck goes crawling in there.

[3] I can hear him somewhere, somewhere close inside of the tree that woodchuck is growling. After all, he had squeezed himself in there. So, there's my ol' dog just barking. "Okay, he slid in there, I think I'm going to put my arm in there to grab on to his tail. I'll pull him out of there real hard, and then my dog will bite him to death," I'm thinking.

[4] So I stick my arm in there wanting to feel around for his tail, and that woodchuck bit me. Aw man, I'm in pain, hollering around there, oh jeez, I take off running home.

[5] Waabanda'ag aw nimaamaayiban, "Nashke-sh indakwamig a'aw akakojiish." "Aaniin danaa endazhiikawad aw akakojiish dakwamik?" Gaa-izhi-wiindamawag gaa-izhichigeyaan, "Mii imaa biinjayi'ii imaa wiimbizid aw mitig, mii imaa gii-shegooded. Imbwaanawi'aa dash imaa da-bi-zaagidooded. Indaano-wii-wiikoobinaa imaa da-giikamaad aw inday."

[6] "Ahaw, gigikendaan ina awiya zegizid, azhetaa. Azhetaa gegoo gotang," indig. "Gii-azhetaa imaa." "Oonh." "Ke inga-gikinoo'amoon ge-izhichigeyan miinawaa ezhiwebak." Wiijiiwid aw mindimooyenh iwidi megwekob, megwayaak. Mii imaa wiimbizid aw chi-mitig, mii imaa gii-poodawed, anooj igo gegoo: aniibiishibagoshan, mashkoshiwishan akina gegoo imaa aw gii-chaagizang imaa. "Shke imaa azhegaabawin," ikido, indig.

[7] Mii dash geget gaa-pi-chi-zaagidooded a'aw akakojiish, mii imaa gaa-tebibinaad aw inday gii-mamigwamaad. "Mii ezhichigeyan, gegoo omaa da-giikanaamozo imaa biindig imaa booch da-zaagidooded."

[8] Wa, mii sa gegoo gii-gikinoo'amawid aw mindimooyenyiban. Geget igo ingii-wiisagininjii igo ginwenzh.

[5] When I show my mom, "Look where I got bit by
a woodchuck." "Why the heck are you messing with a
woodchuck, to have him bite you?" So, I told her what
I had did, "He ran inside the hollow of a tree, he slid
inside there. I couldn't get him to crawl out of there.
I wanted to pull him out of there so my dog could bite
him to death."

[6] "Okay, did you know that when someone is scared,
they back away. They back away when they are scared
of something," she says to me. "He backed away there."
"Oh." "Watch, I'll teach you what to do if that happens
again." She goes with me to the bush, out in the woods.
There at the hollow of that tree, that is where she made
a fire, all kinds of leaves, grass, everything there she
burnt it up in the fire. "Look now, stand back," she says,
she says to me.

[7] And sure enough the woodchuck comes crawling
out real fast and my dog caught him, throwing him all
over with his mouth. "That is what you do, smoke them
out of there, and they'll have to crawl out."

[8] *Wa,* that is something that that old lady taught me.
Aw man, my hand hurt for a long time.

4 Joonya-ish

[1] APANE KO AW BEZHIG NISAYENH, OONH MEWINZHA
igo gii-agaashiinyiyaang, maagizhaa ningo-biboon,
gaa-ningo-biboon... niizho-biboonagiziwaangen wapii,
apane gii-mino-wiiji'idiyaang. Akina gegoo aaniish-naa
ge iniw, mii aw *actually he's my cousin, my first cousin,
but we grew up as brothers.*

[2] Miish aw anooj gegoo gaa-paa-wiijiiwag gii-
izhichigeyaang megwayaak apane ingii-paa-
ayaamin apane go. Mii go mii dash igo azhigwa ani-
dibikaabaminaagwak, gii-kwiishkoshimigooyaang
da-bi-giiweyaang. Ingii-minwendaamin iw megwayaak.

[3] Ingii-kagiibaadiziinsiwimin igo gaye, gaa-oshki-
ininiiwiyaang. Apane ge ingii-pi-wiiji'ayaawidimin,
apane. Apane ge aano-wii-kagwe-aada'wag
awegodogwen igo booch igo da-gagwe-aada'od.

[4] Mii ko bezhig gaa-izhichiged, mii ko iwidi ingoji
gaa-o-izhi-agindang gegoo mazina'igan, miish gomaa
apii gaa-pi-zaagewed miinawaa nanaamadabid,
"Gigikendaan ina o'ow?" "Gaawiin." "Ingikendaan niin."
Ezhi-wiindamawid, "Nashke, ninibwaakaa niin," ko
ikido. Aaniish-naa imaa ogii-o-agindaan imaa, aabita
omazina'iganish wenji-gikendang. Mii ezhichiged a'aw.

 4 Ol' Junior

[1] ONE OF MY OLDER BROTHERS, A LONG TIME AGO WHEN we were little, maybe one year, two years, when we must have been about two years old at the time, we always played well together. Everything, well after all, actually he's my cousin, my first cousin, but we grew up as brothers.

[2] We would do all kinds of things when I went around with him, we were always out in the woods, always. And then, when it started getting real dark out, they would whistle for us to come back home. We loved it out in the woods.

[3] And we were a little bit foolish too, when we were young men. We always lived together, always. Every time I wanted to beat him at something, it didn't matter what it was, he just had to try to outdo me.

[4] Here's one that he did, he would be over there, somewhere reading something in a book, then when he'd come out he'd be sitting there, "Do you know this?" "No." "Well, I do." Then he'd tell me, "See, I am smart, I am," he would always say. He'd go and read it just for the heck of it, half of the book, and that's how he knew it. That's what he did.

[5] Nimikwendaan aabiding imaa chi-
bebezhigooganzhiiwigamig gii-ayaamagad imaa
gii-padakide jiigayi'ii endaayaang, akina dash iw chi-
mazina'igan imaa gii-pakweyaasin. Ezhi-zhiibaayaag
bebezhigooganzhiiwigamig. "Gego ganage wiikaa
baa-akwaandawekegon omaa biindig iw, da-gawaakose
bebezhigooganzhiiwigamig." "Oonh, gaawiin."

[6] Aabiding sa geget gaa-izhi-akwaandaweyaang
baa-dazhitaayaang imaa, endazhi-achigaadeg
iw mashkosiwan, *haymow*, gaa-izhi-waabamag
biidaasamosed iniw, gaa-izhi-waabamimag
biidaasamosenid iniw omaamaayan, gaa-izhi-
niisaandawebatooyaan niin wewiib.

[7] "Aaniish aw *Junior*?" indig. Aabige go geniin
wiindamaageyaan imaa, "Imaa baa-akwaandawe
ishpiming imaa, gii-inad da-akwaandawesig, mii imaa
akwaandawed." Aayay, "*Junior*, bi-niisaandawen omaa!"
Gaa-izhi-gijigwaashkwanid iwidi, ishpimisagong zaagiji-
gwaashkwanid. Ganabaj nising gii-pakite'waad dabwaa-
bangishing omaa mitikamig. Gaa-paa-danaapi'ag imaa,
wiin gii-tebibinaa. Gaawiin niin ingii-tebibinigoosiin.

[8] Miinawaa ge ingiw mitigoog, ingii-waanda-
gikenimaanaanig ingiw mitigoog. Gii-zhawabaagiiyaang
ingiw mitigoog, akwaandaweyaang iwidi, ishpiming
gaa-izhi-maajiibizod aw mitig miinawaa bezhig aw
mitig izhi-nakweyaakwiiyaang, mii miinawaa ezhi-
maminigobinangid miinawaa idi bakaan mitig izhi-
nanaakwiiyaang. Shaa ingii-shawabaagiimin iko, gii-
kwiiwizensiwiyaang.

[5] I remember this one time there was a big barn there, it stood next to our house, but all of the tar paper had blown off. You could see through that barn. "Don't you ever even think about climbing in here, this barn is going to collapse." "Oh, no."

[6] So then this one time of course we climbed up there and were playing there, where they keep the hay, a "haymow," then I saw her walking toward us, I saw his mom walking toward us, so I climbed down real fast in a hurry.

[7] "What about Junior?" she says to me. And I told right away there, "He's climbing around up there, where you told him not to climb, that's where he's climbing." Oh jeez, "Junior, climb down here!" So, he jumps off from there, jumping out from the upstairs area. I think she hit him three times before he fell on the ground. I was cracking up laughing at him; he got caught. It wasn't me who got caught.

[8] And the trees too, we knew the trees really well. We'd jump from tree to tree, climbing around there, up high, then when a tree took off, we catch another tree and climb on it, and when we shake on one, we leap onto another. We used to jump from tree to tree for fun when we were boys.

[9] Noomaya imaa ingii-o-waabamaanaanig ingiw
mitigoog, gaa-akwaandawaanangijig, waanda-
agaashiinyiwag ingiw mitigoog chi-mewinzha dash ko
ingii-inendaamin chi-ishpiming, gii-chi-ginooziwaad
ingiw mitigoog. Gaawiin dash, ingoji go, ingoji go
midaasozid eta go omaa akooziwag.

[10] Gewiin apane gii-pi-ojibwemotawaa gaye wiin,
ogikendaan gewiin iw Ojibwemowin, aw nisayenh.
Miinawaa ge ogichidaawi imaa dewe'iganing,
genawendamaageyaang. Geget ogashkitoon gewiin
azhigwa gaagiigidod, da-ojibwemod. Mii iw.

[9] We saw those trees there recently, the ones we climbed, and those trees are just small, but a long time ago we used to think they were really high, that those trees were real tall. But they're not; they are only about ten feet tall.

[10] Of course they always spoke Ojibwe to him too, he too knows the Ojibwe language, my older brother. He also is an *ogichidaa* on the drum, on the one we take care of for the people. He is capable, too, for when he has to speak, to speak Ojibwe. That's it.

5 Gizhaagamide

[1] MII AW BEZHIG AKIWENZIIYIBAN, MII AW NIZHISHENH ozhishenyibaniin, *my great uncle* ganabaj *Jim Clark's uncle*. Gizhaagamide gii-izhi-wiinaa. Ganabaj nising gii-kibaakwa'waa iwidi chi-gibaakwa'odiwigamigong *Stillwater*. Anooj ko gii-izhichige aw akiwenzii anooj ko gii-inaajimo gaye.

[2] Apane gii-pima'adoo miikanaang chi-miikanaang gii-pima'adood. Meta go meta go gichi-babiinzikawaagan gii-piitookonayed namanj maagizhaa niizhwewaan gaa-piizikawaagwen giboodiyegwaazonan niswewaan. Miinawaa obabiinzikawaaganan maagizhaa niizh, aaniish-naa agwajiing ko gii-nibaa.

[3] Mii dash ko onjida gaa-izhi-gibaakwa'ond, gegoo gaa-ayizhichiged da-gibaakwa'ond da-gawajisig azhigwa imaa biibooninig. Miish imaa aabiding bimosed imaa azhigwa ingoji go gegaa go maadaginzod aw *December*, "Hay' mii azhigwa onzaam gisinaamagak agwajiing da-nibaayaambaan," onendam. Ingii-noondawaa go gii-tibaajimod.

[4] "Enh', aaniin ge-izhichigeyaan? Gegoo inga-izhichige inga-gibaakwa'ogoo dash gabe-biboon miinawaa gaawiin indaa-gawajisiin. Miinawaa ge niwii-minikwe gaye." Mii gaa-izhi-gikendang waa-izhichiged.

5 Hot Water

[1] THIS ONE OLD MAN, HE WAS MY UNCLE'S UNCLE, MY great uncle, I think it was Jim Clark's uncle. They called him *Gizhaagamide* [Hot Water]. I think he did three stints in the Stillwater State Penitentiary. He used to do all kinds of stuff, and he always had some stories to tell.

[2] He was always walking along the road, walking down the highways. He wore a big winter parka with layers on, I don't know how many, maybe three or four pairs of pants. And he had maybe two coats, after all, he would sleep outside.

[3] And he used to get locked up on purpose, doing whatever to get locked up so that he wouldn't freeze to death when it was wintertime. This one time he was walking along, it was around the beginning of December, "Dang, it's too cold out now for me to sleep outside," . . . I heard him tell the story.

[4] "Well, what am I going to do? I'm going to do something; I'm going to get locked up for the winter. I won't freeze to death. Plus, I want to drink too." Then he knew what he was going to do.

[5] Gaa-o-izhi-biindiged imaa *the liquor store*. Gegaa go gaye gii-nitaa-zhaaganaashiimo a'aw akiwenzii, Gizhaagamide. Biindiged imaa *liquor store*, *"May I help you?"* inaa giiwenh. *"Oh just give me a half a gallon of Whiteport."* Mii go imaa badakidamawaa iw *Whiteport*, mii go wewiib gaa-izhi-debibidood baakaakonang chi-maminikwed chi-enigok imaa. *"Hey that'll be..."* namanj gaa-inagindamawaawinden.

[6] Haa miinawaa debibidood imaa chi-minikwed, *"Say you gotta pay for that,"* inaa. *"Gaawiin. I told you to give it to me and you gave it to me,"* ikido. Way, zaagijibatood geyaabi odoomoodaam chi-maminikwed megwaa chi-bimosed iwidi. Aaniish-naa wii-kiiwashkwebii gaye miinawaa wii-takonigozi.

[7] Iwidi gaa-ni-dagoshing idi jiigi-oodena mii iwidi chi-mitigong gii-aatwaakwabid gii-maminikwed. Chi-minikwed, aaniish-naa owii-kidaan iw maanoo da-chi-giiwashkwebiid imaa, mii iw wii-piinjwebinigaazod. Azhigwa-sh igo geget bi-bagamibizowan imaa dakoniwewininiwan. Mii gii-takonind. Mii giiwenh *'defrauding an innkeeper'* giiwenh.

[8] Aaniish-naa gii-inaa, *"gimme"* so he gave it to me. Hay' mii gaawiin, mii gii-takonind. Mii imaa gii-kanawenimind ganabaj *90 days* gii-miinaa. Mii gaa-te-aabawaanig miinawaa apii gii-saaga'ang. Mii gaawiin gii-kawajisiin imaa gaa-pibooninig.

[5] So he goes into the liquor store. That old man could speak pretty good English, that Hot Water. When he went into the liquor store, "May I help you?" they supposedly said to him. "Oh just give me a half of a gallon of Whiteport." They stood the Whiteport up there for him, and he quickly grabbed it, opened it up, and started slamming it, real hard. "Hey, that'll be . . ." I'm not sure how much they charged him.

[6] Then he grabs it again and takes a pull, "Say you gotta pay for that," they said to him. "No. I told you to give it to me and you gave it to me," he said. Then he goes running out, still has his bottle and he's just a slamming on it while he's walking along. After all, he wants to get drunk, and he wants to get arrested.

[7] Then after he gets to the edge of town, he sits down against a tree and drinks his bottle up. He's just slamming it down, naturally, he wants to be tore up when he gets thrown in jail. And now sure enough, the cops come rolling up. He was then arrested. Supposedly it was for defrauding an innkeeper.

[8] "Well, I did say 'gimme,' so he gave it to me." No chance, he was arrested. They took care of him; I think they gave him ninety days. When the weather was warm enough, that is when he came out. He didn't freeze to death during the winter.

6 Gookooko'oo

[1] MIINAWAA GE AABIDING IMAA, MAZHII'IGANING
ezhinikaadeg imaa jiigi-chi-zaaga'iganing imaa, *liquor store* imaa gii-o-biindiged aw Gizhaagamide imaa gaa-izhi-mamood chi-omooday.

[2] Miish imaa gaa-pi-izhaad imaa jiigibiig. Gii-ayaawag ko imaa Anishinaabeg gaa-tazhi-maminikwewaad imaa jiigibiig. Miish gewiin imaa, eyaatwaakwabid imaa chi-mitigong miinawaa, maminikwed, ozhiiginige gaye. Ogii-ayaawaan asemaan miinawaa mazina'igaansan.

[3] Miish gaa-ikidod imaa, "Niganawaabamaa imaa, ishpiming aw chi-mitigong imaa namadabiyaan, nibaad aw gookooko'oo, bizaanabid nibaad imaa. Gaa-izhi-noondawag iwidi opime-ayi'ii akeyaa gewiin imaa aw baa-gwaakwaashkwanid aw chi-misajidamoo, baa-gwaakwaashkwanid imaa anooj imaa mitigong. Maminikweyaan," ikido.

[4] "Ani-ganawaabamag, wayaahay! Eshkam igo besho bi-gwaakwaashkwani aw chi-misajidamoowish, gaa-izhi-bishigwaakwiid. Mii imaa na'idaa imaa nibaanid iniw gookooko'oon gii-pangishing imaa, okweganaang. Gaa-izhi-amazikawaad ini gookooko'oon chi-bazigwa'od aw gookooko'oo. Apane iwidi akeyaa agaami-zaaga'igan, mii iwidi geyaabi ani-minjimaakwiid aw, aw ajidamoowish iwidi akeyaa. Apane gaa-pishkwaabamag."

6 The Owl

[1] AND THEN THERE WAS THIS ONE TIME, OVER IN Garrison along the big lake there, in Garrison, Minnesota, he went into the liquor store there, and he took a big bottle.

[2] Then he came down to the shore. There used to be some Shinaabs that would drink there along the shore. So, he too was sitting there leaning against a big tree and he's just drinking away, rolling a cigarette too. He had tobacco and rolling papers.

[3] Then he says, "I saw an owl sleeping there, way up in that tree as I was sitting there, sitting quietly, sleeping there. Then I heard him over there off to the side, there was a big gray squirrel jumping around, jumping around from tree to tree. While I'm drinking," he says.

[4] "As I am watching him, oh jeez, that ol' gray squirrel was gradually jumping closer and closer, and then he missed a branch. It just so happens that he fell right where that owl was sleeping there, landing on his neck. He woke up that owl, and that owl took off just fast. He was gone, headed toward the other side of the lake, and still holding on was the squirrel over there, then he was gone, and I lost sight of him."

[5] He anishaa gii-ani-nanakweboozid. Mii gaa-
inaajimod. Ogii-tibaajimotawaan dash iniw
ona'aangishiiman. Miish gaye wiin aw bezhig
gaa-ikidod, aaniish-naa anooj gii-ikidowag ingiw
Anishinaabeg, dibaajimotawaad gaa-onaabandang,
"Apane iwidi misajidamoowish gii-nagwaakwiid iwidi
gookooko'ooyan ani-aazhogebizod." "Enh', enh'" ikido
bezhig Anishinaabe, "Ingii-waabamaa biijibizod. Gaye
niin idi agaaming ingii-dazhi-maminikwe iwidi. Ingii-
aatwaakwab gaye imaa mitigong. Ingii-waabamaa aw
chi-gookooko'oo biijibizod. Gegoo go imaa bi-agokeni
imaa opikwanaang. Mii aw misajidamoo gaa-
waabamag."

[5] He had caught a ride for the hell of it. That is how he told the story. He told the story to his in-laws too. Then one of them said, of course the Shinaabs said all kinds of things, when telling stories of what they saw, "He was gone! That gray squirrel that held on to an owl and rode across the water." "Yup, yup," one of those Shinaabs said, "I saw him flying over here. I was on the other side of the lake too drinking over there. And I was sitting against a tree. I saw that big owl come flying. There was something stuck onto his back. It was that gray squirrel that I saw."

7 Biindaakwaan

[1] AKINA INGIW AKIWENZIIYAG GII-PIINDAAKWEWAG
mewinzha. Gii-piindaakwewag mewinzha, miish
aya'aa, indedeyiban, Biidaanimad, miinawaa
nizhishenyiban, Gechiwab gii-izhinikaazo, dibi dash
iwidi gii-minikwewaagwen iwidi akeyaa, besho go
iwidi *Wisconsin, Dairyland, Wisconsin* izhinikaade.
Mii iwidi gii-minikwewaad.

[2] Giiwashkwebiiwag. Ogii-kiiwashkwebiishkaagonaawaa
ko iw zhingobaaboo. "Ahaw, indawaaj izhaadaa iwidi
Ekobiising." *Duxbury* wii-izhaawag. Aah, biijibizowaad
aaniish-naa mii iw, *from east to west* gii-ipizowag iwidi
na'idaa iwidi *west* akeyaa gii-ni-ipizowag ningaabii'anong,
ani-onaagoshig.

[3] Wayaahay ani-bimibizowaad zhigwa ani-dibikad,
gaa-izhi-wanendamowaad imaa *S-curve*. Aaniish-naa
odaabaanishag mewinzha *1930s* gii-ishpagooziwag.
Gaa-izhi-gonabibizowaad imaa ingiw akiwenziiyag.

[4] Wayaa, miish aw indedeyiban, "Waaya, yay, yay,
ingiishkiingweshin omaa nishtigwaaning, wenda-
gawiskwagiziyaan," izhininjiinid iwidi wiin miskwii
gaa-taanginang waanda-bazigwaani. "Oonh yay, aayay
imbiigondibeshin, taawis!"

7 The Chew

[1] ALL OF THOSE OLD MEN CHEWED TOBACCO A LONG TIME ago. They all chewed back then, then um, my dad, Biidaanimad, and my uncle, his name was Gechiwab, I don't know where the hell they were drinking, over there, over there by Wisconsin, it's called Dairyland, Wisconsin. That is where they were drinking.

[2] They were drunk. They used to get drunk on beer. "Alright, how about we head over to Duxbury." They wanted to go to Duxbury. So, they're cruising this way, of course it's, they were driving from east to west, it just happens that it was toward *ningaabii'anong* they were driving, in the evening time.

[3] Oh darn, so as they are driving along, it's now getting dark, they had forgot about that S-curve. Well, the ol' cars back in the 1930s sat real high. Then those old men rolled their car in the ditch.

[4] Oh jeez, then my dad is like, "Oh man, oh wow, ouch, I got a cut on my face here on my head, I'm bleeding bad," as he's touching that blood, it was just sticky. "Aw man, I broke my head, cuz!"

[5] Miish aw nizhishenyiban Gechiwab, "Ahaw
bekaa niitaawis, ishkodens omaa inga-zaka'aan,
inga-waabandaan aaniin ezhi-ishkwagiziyan."
Zaka'ang ishkodens, "Satayaa niijii, zikowinaagan
imaa zikowinaaganish imaa gii-pangisin imaa
gishtigwaaning! Biindaakwaan aw gimiskwiim."

[5] So then my uncle Gechiwab, "Okay, hold on, cuz, I'll
light a match here, I'll see how bad you're bleeding."
He lights a match, "Oh, ick! My friend, a spittoon, that
ol' spittoon fell on your head! That snuff juice is your
blood!"

8 Aano-gii-pakiteganaamid Indedeyiban

[1] AABIDING IMAA JIIGI-ZAAGA'IGAN INGII-TAAMIN, CHI-zaaga'igan igo. Miish apii gaa-izhi-izhaad idi bezhig niwiiji'aagan, "Daga baa-wewebanaabiidaa." "Ahaw goda." Ingoji go ishpi-dibik ingoji go midaaso-diba'iganed, "Niwii-o-wewebanaabiimin imaa Ded," "Ahaw maajaag."

[2] Aaniish-naa mii wiin aabige gii-kawishimod aw akiwenzii. Gaa-izhi-maajaayaang aw niwiiji'aagan, baamishkaayaang idi niibaa-dibik, baa-wewebanaabiiyaang. Aa, gii-waanda-mino-dakaasin iw zaaga'iganing gaawiin ge awiya zagimeg gii-ayaasiiwag.

[3] Miish i'iw gaa-izhi-giizhishing imaa biinji-jiimaaning aw, "Daga nibaadaa omaa gabe-dibik." "Ahaw goda," indinaa. Gaa-izhi-gawishimoyaang imaa jiimaaning imaa michisagokaadeg, wewebanaabiiyaang azhigwa gaa-izhi-nibaayaang.

[4] Chi-gigizheb ko gii-koshkozi aw akiwenziiyiban. Aa, gii-kwiinawaabamid imaa ninibaaganing, gaa-izhi-izhaad iw zaaga'iganing mii iwidi gii-waabandang iw jiimaan dedebagondenig gaawiin awiya gii-zaagikwebisiiwan imaa.

44

8 When My Dad Swung at Me

[1] WE ONCE WERE LIVING BY A LAKE, A RATHER BIG LAKE. So one time, one of my friends came by, "Come on let's go fishing." "Alrighty then." It was late at night sometime around ten o'clock, "We're going to go fishing, Dad." "Alright go on, then."

[2] Well, that old man had already went to lay down. So we headed out, my friend and I, rowing around at night, going around fishing. Oh, it was a nice cool breeze out on the lake, and no mosquitoes were out.

[3] So he got comfortable in the boat and said, "Let's just sleep in the boat all night." "Okay, then," I say to him. So we laid down on the floor of the boat and fell asleep while we were fishing.

[4] That old man used to get up early in the morning. When he didn't see me in my bed, he went to the lake, and that is where he saw the boat floating around with nobody's head sticking up out of it.

[5] Wayaa chi-zegizid chi-baa-biibaagid iwidi.
Ingii-noondawaanaan, ingii-amaji'igonaan dash
ingii-amazomigonaan igo, ingii-amajimigonaan.
Chi-biibaagid gaa-izhi-azhegiiweyaang iwidi.

[6] Mii gegaa gii-pakite'od aw akiwenzii gaa-takonang
mitigoons. "Gego ganage imaa wiikaa miinawaa babaa-
nibaaken imaa jiimaaning imaa. Gigikendaan ina
enaanimiziyaan imaa gwiinawaabaminaan?" "Ahaw."
"Ahaw goda."

[5] Oh, he was scared and was really hollering around out there. We heard him and he woke us up, woke us up by hollering, he woke us up with his voice. He was hollering so we went back over there.

[6] That old man almost hit me with the stick he was carrying. "Don't you ever go sleep out there again out in the boat. Do you know how bad I panicked when I didn't see you out there?" "Okay." "Okay, then."

9 Gaazhagenzhish

[1] GIZHAAGAMIDE GAA-IZHI-IZHAAD IWIDI, GAA-IZHI-IZHAAD iwidi gaa-taanid iniw oshiimeyan. Chi-gigizheb idi gii-ni-dagoshin. Biindiged imaa waakaa'iganing gaawiin awiya gii-ayaasiiwan.

[2] Aah, baamosed imaa biindig, "Mii gaawiin awiya." Mii eta go gaazhagenzhishan imaa bebaamosenijin. Naa gaganoonidizod imaa, "Dibi naa gaa-izhaawaagwen ongow?"

[3] Baamaa go gaazhagenzhish, "*Town!*" "Wa! *Town* iidog izhaawag. Namanj apii gaa-ni-maajaawaagwen uh?" Miinawaa gaazhagenzhish, "*Nine.*" "Namanj ge enanokiiwaagwen iw oodenaang awegodogwen gaa-naadiwaagwen iwidi oodenaang?" "*Wine.*" Ikido, "Mii akina gegoo gii-wiindamawid aw gaazhagenzhish, gii-maajaawag, *town* gii-izhaawag, *nine*, onaadinaawaa *wine*."

9 The Ol' Cat

[1] GIZHAAGAMIDE WENT OVER TO WHERE HIS LITTLE SISTER lived. He arrived early in the morning. When he went into the house there wasn't anybody there.

[2] He was walking around inside, "Nobody here." There was just an old cat who was walking around. He was wondering out loud, "I wonder where they went?"

[3] Pretty soon the cat replied, "Town." "*Wa!* They must have went to town. I wonder what time they headed out?" Again the cat replied, "Nine." "I wonder what their business was in town, I wonder what they had went after?" "Wine." He said, "That old cat told me everything, they left, they went to town, they left at nine, and they went after wine."

10 Noodinoban

[1] AW AKIWENZIIYIBAN GAA-NITAAWIGI'ID APANE KO
ogii-tazhimaan ini bezhig Anishinaaben. Shke mii go
noondang iw bemibideg ishpiming ganawaabandang,
mii ko gaa-ikidod, "Wa! Joe Shabaiash onaanaan
zhooniyaan." Aaniish-naa ingii-kwiiwizensiw, "Awegwen
naa Joe Shabaiash naanaagwen zhooniyaan?" Gomapii
miinawaa azhigwa idi bimibideg bezhig, "Wa! Na!
Mii gii-naanaad Joe Shabaiash zhooniyaan." Meta
go gaa-ikidod. Gaawiin ge gegoo gii-ikidosiin aw
mindimooyenh.

[2] Miinawaa ge ko o-nandawaabandang ow
ozhooniyaa-mazina'igan imaa azhigwa bagamibidenig,
"Wa! Joe Shabaiash imbi-izhinizha'amaag
zhooniyaansan. Ambe oodenaang izhaadaa!"
"Awegwen naa aw Joe Shabaiash?" ko indinendam.

[3] "Aah Joe Shabaiash imbi-izhinizha'amaag
zhooniyaan. Ahaw. Oodenaang izhaadaa!" Mii go ko
ge gii-o-adaawed gegoo waa-miijiyaang izhaad idi
adaawewigamigong. "Joe Shabaiash ingii-adaawetamaag
iniw akina gegoo wiisiniwin akina gegoo imaa ingii-
adaawetamaag."

10 Joe Shabaiash

[1] THAT OLD MAN THAT RAISED ME WOULD ALWAYS TALK about this one Shinaab. You see, when he heard a plane flying by in the sky he would look at it, and then he'd say, "*Wa!* Joe Shabaiash is going after money." After all, I was just a little boy, "Who is this Joe Shabaiash that is going after money?" Then eventually another one would come by, "*Wa!* See! Joe Shabaiash has gone after money." That's all he would say. That old lady didn't say anything.

[2] And also when he would go out and look for his check, then when it would come, "*Wa!* Joe Shabaiash sent me a little bit of money. Come on let's go to town!" I used to think, "Who the heck is this Joe Shabaiash?"

[3] "Ah, Joe Shabaiash sent me money. Okay. Let's go to town!" Then he would go and buy everything that we wanted to eat over at the store. "Joe Shabaiash bought me all of the food, Joe Shabaiash bought me everything."

[4] Genapii go, "Wayaahay meno-bimaadizid aw
Joe Shabaiash," indinendam. Ingwiiwizensiw dash,
nabaj ingoji go ingii-ningodwaaso-biboonagiz. Mii
azhigwa dash igo ingoding gaa-o-izhi-aanjidaabaaned
bagamibizod imaa endaayaang gii-aanjidaabaaned aw
akiwenziiyiban o-zaagijibatooyaang o-waabamangid
aw odaabaan, waanda-onaajiwi.

[5] "Enh'! Joe Shabaiash ingii-adaawetamaag
odaabaanan idi oodenaang." Aayay! "Mii meno-
bimaadizid aw Joe Shabaiash." Wayaahay, aaniish-
naa gaawiin ge akeyaa ingii-waabamaasiin aw Joe
Shabaiash. Akina gegoo gaa-ayaang, Joe Shabaiash
ogii-adaawetamaagoon.

[6] Gaa-izhi-waabamag azhigwa go maagizhaa
gaa-shaangaso-biboonagiziwaanen midaaso-
biboonagiziwaanen. Mii ko gaa-pi-ikidod apane, "Joe
Shabaiash ingii-adaawetamaag. Joe Shabaiash ingii-pi-
izhinizha'amaag mazina'iganan." Gaa-izhi-waabamag
ingoding, gaganoonaad iniw bezhig anishinaaben
aw akiwenzii, gaa-izhi-gagwejimag aw nimaamaa,
"Wenesh a'aw maa?" "Aa mii a'aw Joe Shabaiash."
Eni-waawaabamag, oonh yay!

[7] Nawaj iniw odoodaabaanan gii-maanaadiziwan
apiish niinawind indoodaabaaninaan. Wayaa waanda-
gidimaagizi ko ge aw akiwenzii. Gii-paataniinowan
ini oniijaanisan. "Namanj naa wenji-gashkitoogwen
da-adaawetamawaad iniw akiwenziiyan akina gegoo
odaabaanan, zhooniyaan?" ingii-ondamendam.

[4] Then eventually, "Oh jeez that Joe Shabaiash is living the good life," I thought. I was just a little boy; I think I was around six years old. Then one time when he got a different car, he drove up to our house having gotten a different car, and we'd all run outside to go see the car; it was real nice.

[5] "Yes! Joe Shabaiash bought me a car in town." For crying out loud! "That Joe Shabaiash is living the good life." Oh jeez, after all, I had never seen that Joe Shabaiash before. Everything that he had Joe Shabaiash had bought for him.

[6] And then I saw him, must have been maybe when I was nine or ten years old. He would always say to us, "Joe Shabaiash bought it for me. Joe Shabaiash sent me the checks." Then I saw him one time; that old man was talking to this one Anishinaabe, so I asked my mom, "Who is that, Mom?" "Oh that's Joe Shabaiash." So I'm looking him over, oh lordy!

[7] He had a more ugly car than we did. Oh that old man was just raggedy. He had a whole bunch of kids. "I wonder how the heck he was able to buy that old man everything, a car, money," I thought.

[8] Gaa-izhi-gagwejimag aw mindimooyenyiban, "Aaniish apane wenji-adaawetamoonang aw Joe Shabaiash odaabaanan miinawaa zhooniyaansan bi-izhinizha'amawaad adaawetamoonang odaabaanan akina gegoo?" "Yay! Gego bizindawaaken aw akiwenzhiiyish," ikido indedeyan. "Aaniish goda wenji-ikidod iw?" "Oonh ingiw wewiitaayijig omamiikwaazomaawaan iniw wiitaawaan, ingiw anishinaabeg ininiwag, mii ezhichigewaad. Anishaa ikidowag mamiikwaanaawaad iniw owiitaawaan. Mii iniw wiitaan iniw Joe Shabaiash." "Oonh!"

[9] Miish iw bakaan gaa-izhi-inenimag Joe Shabaiash. Mii ekwaabiigak i'iw gaa-mino-bimaadizid Joe Shabaiash.

[8] So then I asked that old lady, "How come Joe Shabaiash always buys us cars and sends us money, buys cars for us and everything?" "Oh jeez don't listen to that old man," she said about my dad. Why did he say that? "Oh, they're brothers-in-law, Anishinaabe men brag about their brothers-in-law, that's what they do. They just say things jokingly when they brag about their brothers-in-law. That's his brother-in-law, Joe Shabaiash." "Oh!"

[9] I then thought differently about Joe Shabaiash. That's it for that one, about Joe Shabaiash, the great one.

11 Gaa-shizhookang Akiwenzii

[1] ANOOJ KO GII-IZHICHIGEWAG INGIW ANISHINAABEG.
Anooj ogii-toodawaawaan iniw owiitaawaan. Shke
iw indedeyiban ingii-waabamaa gaa-toodawaad iniw
owiitaan. Megwaa giiwoseyaang, gaawiin mashi goon
gii-ayaasiin. Mii dash aw akiwenziiyiban gaa-izhi-ikidod,
"Tayaahay!" ikido. "Aapiji niwii-miizii omaa." Miish imaa
gaa-izhaad imaa bangii imaa awas gaa-o-danashkadizod.

[2] Azhigwa miinawaa biidaasamose gaa-kiizhiitaad.
Gii-waanda-bangan, gaa-izhi-izhinoo'ang obaashkizigan
ishpiming gaa-izhi-madweziged. "Aaniish naa wenji-
izhichigeyan, Ded?" indinaa. "Bekaa."

[3] Gaa-izhi-biibaagimaad iniw wiitaan iwidi besho
gii-akandoowan, "Gus omaa bi-izhaan, Gus, wewiib!
Waah, biidaasamoseshid aw akiwenzii iniw wiitaan,
"Wegonen da?" "Gidaa-waabamaa na giin a'aw?
Ganabaj nimaakinawaa, ganabaj nimiikonawaa a'aw."
"Aandi?" "Omaa akeyaa bangii nawaj izhaan iwidi
akeyaa miish idi akeyaa ge-inaabiyan."

[4] Animosed aw akiwenzii, "Bekaa nawaj azhedakokiin
imaa bangii. Mii gegaa imaa anooj imaa inaabin imaa."

56

11 When the Old Man Stepped in Crap

[1] THE ANISHINAABE USED TO DO ALL KINDS OF STUFF. They did all kinds of things to their brothers-in-law. See, once I saw what my dad did to his brother-in-law. While we were hunting, there wasn't any snow yet. Then the old man said, "Oh no! I really have to take a crap here." So he went a little further out of the way there to where he took his crap.

[2] Now he's walking back toward us having finished. It was really quiet, so then he pointed his gun in the air and fired it. "Why are you doing that, Dad?" I said to him. "Hold on."

[3] So then he hollered out to his brother-in-law who was waiting close by, "Gus, come here, Gus, hurry up!" *Waah,* when his brother-in-law, that old man was hobbling up to us, "What the heck?" "Can you see him? I think I hit him. I think I wounded him." "Where?" "Over this way a little more, go over that way and look in that direction."

[4] As the old man walked away, "Step back a little more. Right about there, look all over there."

[5] Mii imaa gii-wiindamawaad da-o-niibawinid imaa gii-miiziid. Miish aw akiwenziiyiban akina gegoo baa-izhi-dakokaadang iw moo. Akina go iniw omakizinan gaa-izhi-moowiwaninig. Mii iw apii gaa-paashkaapid aw indedeyiban, "Aayay! Gigii-shizhookam imaa gii-miiziiyaan." "Wayaa! Onjida gidoodaw iw!"

[5] That is where he told him to go stand, where he had taken a crap. That is where that old man was stepping all over in the crap. His shoes had crap all over them. That is when my old man busted out laughing, *"Aayay!* You stepped on my crap!" *"Wayaa!* You did that to me on purpose!"

12 Ishpidoondinechigewag

[1] MEWINZHA KO INGII-NOONDAWAAG INGIW INDEDEYIBAN
miinawaa iniw owiiji'aaganan, anooj ko ayikidowaad.
Miish apane ko gaa-ikidowaad, "Niijii, izhaadaa oodi
Odaawaa-zaaga'iganing. "Ahaw, izhaadaa iwidi." Eko-
baapiwaad. Namanj igo gaa-onji-ikidowaagwen. Apane
go waabandiwaad, "Enh'! Odaawaa-zaaga'iganing
izhaadaa, ishpidoondinechigewag ingiw ikwewag iwidi.
Geget igo ge maminogaamowag."

[2] Eko-baapiwaad iko. Miish geget ingoding iidog a'aw
gaa-azhe-izhaad a'aw bezhig omaa Misi-zaaga'iganing idi
Anishinaabe. Mii gii-mikawaad iniw bezhig Odaawaa-
zaaga'iganii-ikwen, gii-piinaad Misi-zaaga'iganing omaa.
"Wayaa gii-izhaa niitaawis eyaawaad iniw Odaawaa-
zaaga'iganii-ikwen. Wa! Ishpidoondinichige gaye aw
ikwe."

[3] Ingii-waabamaa idi aw ikwe baa-agoojiged
agoodood ani-giziibiiga'iged imaa. Geget ko gii-
ishpidoondinechige. Mii dash igo ingoding gii-
ishkwaa-niibing ingii-waabamaa aw ikwe. Mii akina
gii-pakwesidood iniw ishpidoondinechiganan. Haa
nawaj igo ge gii-ni-bakaakadozo. Mii gii-inigaa'aad
iniw Odaawaa-zaaga'iganii-ikwen. Miinooj ko idi
gii-ikidowaad, "Odaawaa-zaaga'iganing izhaadaa.
Ishpidoondinechigewag ingiw ikwewag."

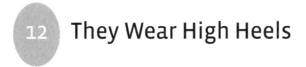

12 They Wear High Heels

[1] A LONG TIME AGO, I USED TO HEAR MY DAD AND HIS friends, oh they'd say all kinds of things. There is one thing they always used to say, "Niijii, let's go to LCO [Lac Courte Oreilles Reservation]." "Okay, let's go then." They'd laugh like hell. I don't know why they would always say that. When they would see one another, "Hey, let's go to LCO. Those women wear high heels over there. They're just nice and plump too."

[2] They used to laugh like hell. So sure enough, one time this one Shinaab from here at Mille Lacs came back from over there. He had found an LCO woman and brought her here to Mille Lacs. "Holy smokes my cousin went over there; he's got an LCO woman, she wears high heels too."

[3] I saw the woman over there hanging out clothes; she was doing laundry. Yup, she was wearing high heels. And then one time, when the summer was over, I saw that woman. She had broken all of her high heels off. And she was getting rather skinny. Here he was terrible to that LCO woman. Nevertheless, they'd say, "Let's go to LCO. Those women wear high heels."

13 Manoomin Naa Ogookomisan

[1] INGIW ANISHINAABEG MEWINZHA BAATANIINOWAG GAA-nitaawigi'igojig iniw ogookomisiwaan. Miish aw bezhig niwiiji-minikwemaagan, naanoomaya gaa-maajaad, Manoomin ko gii-izhi-wiinaa. Ogii-nitaawigi'igoon iniw ogookomisan.

[2] Mii aw akiwenziiyiban gaa-nitaawigi'id mii iniw owiiyawen'enyan, Biidaanimad wiin go gii-izhinikaazo. Miish aw 'Manoomin' gaa-aabajitood apane. Iidog imaa gii-taa imaa jiigi-ziibi aw mindimooyenyiban nigezikwenimaag aw, imaa gii-taawaad mii imaa gaa-nitaawigid aw Manoomin, jiigayi'ii imaa gaawiin waasawasinoon imaa *Grantsburg, Wisconsin.*

[3] Mii dash gaawiin gii-odoodaabaanisiiwag. Gaawiin gii-odoodaabaanisiiwag mewinzha. Apane gii-anookiid aw mindimooyenh da-izhiwinind adaawewigamigong. Ogii-minwendaan ko gaye gii-maminikwed, izhaad adaawewigamigong oodenaang izhaad.

[4] Miish sa aabiding dibi gaa-ondinaawaagwen maagizhaa gaa-adaawegwen aw akiwenziiyiban, iniw odaabaanan. Gii-noonde-ishkwaa-ayaa dash aw ganabaj aw akiwenzii, odakiwenziimibaniin. Mii dash aw Manoomin iniw ogramaayan ogookomisan, "Indaga, Manoomin nitaa-odaabii'iwen, gagwejidaabii'iwen." "Haa gaawiin sha ninitaa-odaabii'iwesiin!" "Haa! Gojichigen! Booch igo gojichigeyan! Shke giga-izhiwizh oodenaang ingoding nitaa-odaabii'iweyan."

62

13 Manoomin and His Grandma

[1] THERE WERE A LOT OF SHINAABS A LONG TIME AGO WHO were raised by their grandmothers. Everybody was raised by their grandmother. So one of my old drinking partners, who recently passed, they used to call him Manoomin. He was raised by his grandmother.

[2] That was a namesake of the old man who raised me, his name was Biidaanimad. But he always used the name Manoomin. That old lady must have lived by the river, I barely remember her, they lived there, and that is where Manoomin grew up, right by there, not far from Grantsburg, Wisconsin.

[3] And they didn't have a car. They didn't have cars a long time ago. That old lady would always hire someone to take her to the store. She liked to drink too, when she went to the store, when she went to town.

[4] Then this once time, I don't know where they got a car, maybe that old man had bought it. I think that old man had just unexpectedly passed away. So Manoomin's gramma, his grandmother is like, "Come on, Manoomin, drive good, learn how to drive." "Jeez, I don't know how to drive!" "Aah! Try to! You have to try! See, you will bring me to town once you can drive good."

[5] "Ahaw," odinaan. Miish ko imaa Manoomin baa-
gagwejibizod imaa, eshkam igo waasa babaamibizo,
baa-wiidabimigod iniw mindimooyenyan. Gaawiin gii-
nitaa-zhaaganaashiimosiin aw mindimooyenh. Miish
ko miish ko babaamibizowaad meta go gaa-inaad iniw
Manoominiyan, "Meta go pwaadii ge-apiichibizoyan!
Meta go pwaadii!" Gaawiin gii-nitaa-ikidosiin iw *forty.*
"Meta go pwaadii epiichibizoyan, Manoomin! Gego
ganage gizhiibizoken!" "Ahaw." Babaamibizowaad imaa,
meta go pwaadii.

[6] Aah ingoding dash mewinzha gii-nitaa-odaabii'iwed
aw Manoomin, ingoding iniw mindimooyenyan gaa-
izhi-ganoonigod, "Indaga, izhaadaa oodi oodenaang."
Mii iidog oodi *Grantsburg.* "Izhiwizhishin iwidi.
Baa-odaabii'iwen, Manoomin!" "Ahaw." Gaa-ni-
maajiibizowaad, "Meta go pwaadii, Manoomin, meta
go pwaadii ge-apiichibizoyan! Gego gizhiikaaken! Meta
go pwaadii." Izhinoo'iged aw mindimooyenyiban imaa,
"Meta go pwaadii ge-apiichibizoyan!" "Ahaw, ahaw!"

[7] Gaa-tagoshinowaad iw oodenaang, babaa-biindiged
aw mindimooyenh adaawewigamigoon baa-ayadaawed.
Baa-wiijiiwaad iniw ogookomisan gaa-izhi-biindiged
aw mindimooyenh imaa ziiginigewigamigong. Haa
maminikwed imaa, aaniish-naa Chi-mookomaanan ge
ogii-mina'igoon aw mindimooyenh anooj igo gegoo
menikwed.

[5] "Okay," he says to her. So there is Manoomin, practic-ing driving there, and he's gradually driving further and further, with that old lady riding shotgun. She didn't speak English very well. So they'd be out driving, and all that she would say to Manoomin is, "Only forty miles per hour! Only drive forty!" She couldn't really say "forty." "Only drive forty, Manoomin! Don't even think about driving fast!" "Okay." So they're cruising around, only forty.

[6] Then this one time, after Manoomin had already learned to drive a long time ago, that old lady called him one time, "Come on, let's go out to town." It must have been over there in Grantsburg. "Bring me over there. You drive, Manoomin!" "Alright." After they had taken off, "Only go forty, Manoomin, only drive forty miles per hour! Don't go fast! Only forty." That old lady would point there, "Only go forty miles an hour!" "Okay, okay!"

[7] When they had got to town, that old lady was going around to stores, buying different things. As he was going around with his grandma, that old lady goes into a bar, she's drinking away in there, and of course the white guys are in there giving her all kinds of drinks.

[8] Miinawaa dash igo maazhaa gaa-kiizhibiigwen aw
mindimooyenh, "Ahaw, Manoomin! Ani-giiwedaa!
Indaakoshkadeshkaagon iw gaa-minikeyaan omaa."
"Ahaw goda boozin." Namanj apii gaa-taawaagwen
imaa gaa-apiichaagwen, "Ahaw, indaga, Manoomin.
Nawaj bangii gizhiibizon! Gegoo indinamanji' imaa
nimisadaang!" "Hay' gaawiin, *Gram*, meta go pwaadii!"
"Gaawiin, Manoomin nawaj gizhiikaan! Ganabaj niwii-
saaga'am aapiji." "Naa gaawiin, *Gram*. Meta go pwaadii
gaa-izhiyan meta go pwaadii ge-apiichibizoyang."
"Aayay, Manoomin! Wewiibitaan, gizhiikaan!" Mii sa
go gaawiin aw Manoomin. Meta go pwaadii.

[9] I'iwapii gaa-tagoshinowaad imaa endaawaad
chi-maajiibatood chi-gabaagwaashkwanid
aw mindimooyenh imaa odaabaaning chi-
mawinadwaadang iw miiziiwigamig agaawaa gii-
pagamibatoo. Iwidi madwetood imaa miiziiwigamigong.
Miish imaa aw Manoomin endanaapi'idizod imaa idi
baapi'aad iniw mindimooyenyan imaa.

[10] Azhigwa bi-zaagewe aw mindimooyenh, "Aayay yay
yay, Manoomin eniwek sa go omaa meji-izhiwebiziyan!
Onjida gidoodaw iw, Manoomin! Gegaa imaa
gegaa imaa ninoonde-zaaga'am." Chi-animosed chi-
giikaamigod iniw ogramaayibaniin, "Aaniish-naa Gram,
meta go pwaadii!" Meta go iw.

[8] So now after she is finished drinking, "Alright, let's go home, Manoomin. Whatever I drank gave me a belly-ache." "Okay then, get in the car." I don't know how far away they lived from there. "Okay, please drive a little bit faster! I feel something in my stomach!" "Darn, no Gram, only forty!" "No, Manoomin, go faster! I think I have to go to the bathroom bad." "Nope, Gram, you told me only forty, we only go forty miles an hour." "Christ, Manoomin! Hurry up, go fast!" But Manoomin didn't. Only forty.

[9] Then when they had arrived there at their house that old lady took off running just fast, jumping out of the car there, really charging toward the outhouse, she barely made it in time. There she was heard doing her business in the bathroom. So there's Manoomin cracking up at himself there, laughing at that old lady.

[10] When that old lady came back around the corner, "Oh jeez, Manoomin, you're evil! You did this to me on purpose, Manoomin! I almost, almost went too early!" He walks off real fast as his grandma is just arguing with him, "Well actually, Gram, *meta go pwaadii* [only go forty]!"

14 Baa-gaanjwebinamaan Ninibaagan

[1] INGII-ADAAWANGEMIN AABIDING WAAKAA'IGAN IMAA, jiigayi'ii imaa-sh Gaa-zhiigwanaabikokaag, Mayaami-ziibiing. Mii eta go iw jiibaakwewigamig miinawaa iw abiiwigamig miinawaa, miinawaa imaa gii-ayaamagad ninibewigamig. Gaawiin dash ishkwaandem gii-ayaamagasinoon imaa nibewigamigong. Mii iwidi mizhisha abiitawind ninibaagan gii-ateg.

[2] Gaa-izhi-bawaajigeyaan iidog, bimibizoyaang. Niwiidabimaa imaa bezhig inini niigaan odaabaaning. Miinawaa ingiw ikwewag idi, ikwezensag iwidi ishkweyaang namadabiwag. Baamibizoyaang, baa-minikweyaang, wayaahay miinawaa chi-gizhiibizoyaan gaye, gegaa ningodwaak indapiichibiz.

[3] Ganawaabandamaan iw epiichibizod aw odaabaan, mii zhigwa gegaa ningodwaak, chi-ogidaakiiwebizoyaang imaa. Miish imaa na'idaa imaa chi-washkamog. "Heyaa!" indinaag, "Gibitaakoshinimin omaa. Minjimaakwiig omaa anaamayi'ii imaa aadikwe'iganing imaa," "Ahaw!" "Minjimaakwiig, enigok!"

68

14 Pushing My Bed Around

[1] WE RENTED A HOUSE ONE TIME HERE, ON THE OUTSKIRTS of Hinckley, in Cloverdale, Minnesota. There was only a kitchen and a living room and there was my bedroom. But there wasn't a door to my bedroom. My bed was in the next room, right out in plain sight.

[2] So I must have been dreaming, that we were driving along. I was sitting up front in the car with a man. And there were women, some girls sitting in the back there. We're driving around, going around drinking, oh jeez, and we're cruising just fast, I'm driving almost a hundred miles an hour.

[3] As I look to see how fast the car is going, it is now going almost a hundred, and we're driving up a big hill there. It just so happens to be, coincidentally that there is a big curve in the road. "Heyaa!" I say to them, "We're crashing here! Brace yourselves under the dashboard!" "Okay!" "Hold on tight!"

[4] Mii eta go chi-baapiwaad ingiw ishkweyaang
nemadabijig imaa. Aa, chi-enigok imaa
minjimaakwiiyaan gegaa go gaanjida'wag a'aw
odaabaan imaa epiichibizoyaang. Gaa-izhi-
amajiseyaan.

[5] Ingwana go naa ningaanjida'aan iw ninibaagan.
Mii eta go biitooshkiganag baazikawagwaa. Ingiw dash
gaa-paapijig imaa ishkweyaang, mii iwidi ishkweyaang
akeyaa, gii-pi-mawadishiwewaad iidog ingiw ikwewag
gii-pi-waabamaawaad iniw nimaamaayibaniin.

[6] Mii ingwana ingiw gaanjida'amaan nibaagan,
mii ingiw nemadabiwaad, chi-gaginagaapiwaad,
baapi'iwaad imaa. Aaniish-naa, gaawiin gegoo
ishkwaandem gii-ayaamagasinoon imaa.

[4] The ones in the back seat are just cracking up laughing. So, I'm bracing myself too, almost pushing the car we're going so fast. And then I wake up.

[5] Here it turns out that I'm pushing my bed. I'm wearing just my underwear. The ones who were laughing in the back, there in the back, they must have been those women over to visit; they were there to see my mom.

[6] It turns out I'm pushing my bed and they were sitting there, giggling away, laughing at me there. After all, there was no door to my room.

15 Megwayaak

[1] AHAW, NASHKE MEWINZHA AW GAA-NITAAWIGI'ID akiwenzii, akiwenziiyiban, ingoji go gii-niso-biboonagiziyaan ingii-maajii-baa-wiijiiwaa iwidi megwayaak, anooj gegoo gii-paa-izhichiged, nashke gegoo wiin wawaaj ge gii-wanii'iged, miinawaa gii-manised. Akina gegoo, geshkitooyaan da-wiijiiwag.

[2] Anooj ko gegoo ingii-paa-waabanda'ig imaa megwayaak, iniw ge zayaagakiigin, miinawaa ingiw mitigoog. Mii go gaa-paa-waabanda'id, "Nashke ingwis," gii-ikido. "Mii iw..." izhinoo'ang imaa gegoo, "Mii iw wenizhishing awiya aakozid, gegoo enamanji'od. Mii iw wenizhishing o'ow dinowa."

[3] Aah, baamosed iko miinawaa, "Aah nashke giwaabamaa na aw mitig?" Mii aw mitig ko bekwe'ond, "Mii ge wenizhishing awiya gegoo inaapined." Akina gegoo ingii-paa-waabanda'ig, apane baa-wiijiiwag, biinish igo gii-oshkinawewiyaan.

72

15 Out in the Woods

[1] OKAY, WELL, A LONG TIME AGO THAT OLD MAN THAT raised me, who is no longer with us, when I was about three years old, I started to go along with him out in the woods, he'd go around doing all kinds of things, see he even went trapping, and he cut firewood. And for all of it, I was able to go along with him.

[2] He went around showing me all kinds of things out there in the woods, the plants, and the trees. When he'd be taking me around showing me things he'd say, "Check this out son." "That's . . ." as he pointed at something there, "This is good for when someone is sick, for when they feel a certain way, that is what this kind is good for."

[3] So, he'd be walking around and again, "Look, you see that tree?" There would be a tree there with a piece of bark taken off, "This is good for when a person has a certain type of sickness." He went around showing me everything, all the time when I went with him, until I reached my adolescence.

[4] Aah, aabiding dash, gaa-ininiiwiyaan, aaniish-naa chi-oodenaang ingii-paa-daa, ingii-paa-daa mewinzha. Gaa-izhi-ishkwaa-ayaad a'aw akiwenzii. Gaa-izhi-azhegoziyaan imaa Aazhoomog, gii-o-wiij'ayaawag aw mindimooyenh gaa-nitaawigi'id, gii-nazhikewizi.

[5] Ingoding igo aabiding imaa odaabaan bi-noogishkaa imaa, jiigayi'ii waakaa'iganing. Gabaawaad ingiw, chi-aya'aawiwag igo, bi-biindiged a'aw akiwenzii miinawaa mindimooyenh. Nanaamadabiwaad imaa, gomaapii-sh gaa-izhi-gagwejimid a'aw akiwenzii, aano-wii-ininamawid asemaan, "Gidaa-naadin ina iwidi megwayaak o'ow?" Namanj gaa-izhinikaadamogwen.

[6] "Miinawaa o'ow bezhig dinowa," namanj gaa-izhinikaadang, "Gidaa-naadinan na? Inga-biindaakoonin inga-miinin zhooniyaa." "Aah, gaawiin ingikendanziin, awegonen dinowa i'iw." Chi-ganawaabamid a'aw mindimooyenh gaa-nitaawigi'id, "Gaawiin ina gigikendanziin iw?" "Gaawiin ingikendanziin." "Oonh. Awiya bakaan gidaa-o-gagwejimaa," ikido a'aw mindimooyenh gaa-nitaawigi'id.

[7] Mii gii-mawadisidiwaad, miish imaa gaa-ni-izhi-maajaawaad. Mii imaa wapii gii-naniibikimid aw mindimooyenh gaa-nitaawigi'id. "Mii imaa gaa-paa-onji-izhiwinik aw akiwenzii megwayaak apane gii-paa-ayaad. Mii gaa-paa-onji-gikinoo'amook akina gegoo enaabadadinig. Nashke dash omaa, noongom omaa awiya bi-izhaad, mii gaawiin gigikendanziin. Aaniin da ezhiwebiziyan?" Ingii-naniibikimig.

[4] So then this one time, after I had become a man, well, I was out living down in the [Twin] Cities, I lived all over the place back then. Then that old man passed away. So I moved back to *Aazhoomog*, and moved in with that old lady who had raised me, she was all alone.

[5] Then this one time a car stopped by there, next to the house. When they got out of the car, they were rather elderly, that old man and old lady came inside. They were sitting there, and eventually that old man asks me, wanting to give me tobacco, "Can you go get this out in the woods?" I don't know what the heck he called it.

[6] "And this kind too." I don't know what he called it, "Can you go get them? I'll offer you tobacco and give you some money." "Aah, I don't know what kind that is." That old lady that raised me is just glaring at me, "You don't know?" "I don't know." "Oh." "You should go ask someone else," that old lady that raised me said.

[7] So they visited for a while, and then they headed out. That is when that old lady that raised me really scolded me. "That is why that old man always brought you along with him out in the woods when he would go out there. He was taking you around teaching you how everything is used on people. Now you see, when someone comes here, you don't even know it. What the heck is the matter with you?" She really scolded me.

[8] Mii ingwana gaa-paa-onji-wiijiiwag aw akiwenzii, gaa-paa-onji-wiijiiwid, aw gii-gikinoo'amawid akina gegoo. Mii iw gaawiin ingii-pizindawaasiin aw akiwenzii, onzaam ingii-ondamiz niin megwayaak gii-paa-dazhitaayaan, anooj gegoo baa-waawaabandamaan. Gaawiin ingii-pizindawaasiin. Mii wenji-apiitendaagwak iw awiya da-bizindawad, gikinoo'amook gegoo. Mii gomaa minik ezhi-mikwendamaan gii-naniibikimid aw mindimooyenh.

[9] Shke, indayaawaag ingozisag, indayaawaag ongow, gii-ishwaachiwag ingozisag. Ganabaj niizh egaashiinyijig nawaj a'aw Miskobineshiinh miinawaa aw mayaamawi-abinoojiinyiwid a'aw Giiwitaayaanimad. Mii aw Giiwitaayaaniimad miinawaa Miskobineshiinh ko ingii-paa-wiijiiwaag gii-paa-giiwoseyaan, gikinoo'amawagwaa o'ow akeyaa ge-izhichigewaad giiwosewaad. Mii ge a'aw, Giiwitaayaanimad aw egaashiinyid, mii aw menwendang giiwosed. Gii-niso-biboonagizi gii-paa-waawiijiiwid idi megwayaak, gii-gikinoo'amawag da-nandokawechiged, da-nandokawe'aad waawaashkeshiwan. Geget minwendam baa-giiwosed a'aw. Gegoo oga-gikendaan naagaj.

[10] Nashke ge a'aw, gwiiwizens, ingozis, nitaa-nagamo gaye. Zhaagwenimo dash wii-nagamod. Akina gegoo onagamonan mii go bizindang iniw nagamonan, mii go eni-ina'ang ezhi-gikendang, shaa go niizhing nising noondang, mii go gii-gikendang. Nimbizindawaa ko odaabaaning nagamod naa imaa onibewigamigong nagamod ko. Miinawaa ge idi aaningodinong iniw mide-nagamonan ge omiikwa'aanan, gii-paa-izhaad iwidi endazhi-midewing. Niibowa ogikendaanan iniw nagamonan, zhaagwenimo dash wii-nagamod.

[8] It turns out that is why I always went along with that old man, why he was always with me, teaching me about everything. I didn't listen to that old man, because I was too busy out in the woods playing around, checking out all kinds of things. I wasn't listening to him. That is why it is important for you to listen to someone, when they are teaching you something. That is all I remember about when that old lady scolded me.

[9] See, I have sons, I had eight sons. There are two of the younger ones, *Miskobineshiinh* and the youngest is *Giiwitaayaanimad*. It's always *Giiwitaayaanimad* and *Miskobineshiinh* that I went with when I would go around hunting, teaching them how they should do things when they hunt. It is him, my youngest *Giiwitaayaanimad,* he is the one who really likes hunting. He was three when he started hunting with me out in the woods, when I taught him about tracking, to track deer. Oh yeah, he likes to hunt that one. That is something he will know later on.

[10] You see, it is him, that boy, my son, he is a good singer too. But he is shy about it when it comes to singing. All the songs, he listens to them all, then he sings them how he knows them, after hearing them only two or three times, then he knows them. I always listen to him singing in the car and there in his bedroom, he always sings. Sometimes too, over there, he'll come out with Mide songs from when he went over to where they do Midewiwin. He knows lots of songs, but he is bashful about singing them.

[11] Pegizh wiikaa wanendanzig iniw nagamonan,
pegizh ani-nitaa-nagamod. Miinawaa ge pegizh
igo ani-nitaa-ojibwemod. Indoojibwemotawaa ko
omaa ayaayaang. Miish ongow aanind gaawiin
indoojibwemotawaasiwaanaanig. Aaniish-naa gaawiin
ge wiinawaa ogikendanziinaawaa. Ingii-wanichige
niin, iw gii-gikinoo'amawaasiwagwaa ingiw ingozisag.
Aaniish-naa gaawiin akina ingii-nitaawigi'aasiig, ingii-
nitaa-bami'aasiig. Mii omaa minik ezhi-wiindamoonaan.

[11] I hope he never forgets those songs, I hope he turns into a good singer. And I hope that he learns to speak good Ojibwe. I always speak Ojibwe to him when we are together. Some of them we do not speak Ojibwe to. After all, they do not know it. I made that mistake, by not teaching that to my sons. After all, I didn't raise them all; I wasn't good at providing for them. That is all I want to tell you.

Wiidookawishin!

[1] AABIDING BAA-MINIKWEYAAN IMAA CHI-OODENAANG, gaa-izhi-nakweshkawag a'aw bezhig niitaawis, aah, ziiginigewigamigong. Haa, mii zhigwa gegaa gibaakwa'igaadeg, wii-kibaakwa'igaadeg. Gaa-izhi-adaaweyaang zhingobaaboo da-ni-maajiidooyaang. Zhigwa gaa-kibaakwa'igaadeg mii zhigwa maajiibizoyaang.

[2] "Aandish ge-izhaayang?" "Oo, imaa," ikido, "Imaa jiigi-ziibiing imaa *Mississippi*. Ayaamagad imaa, besho iniw adoopowinan. Mii imaa ge-o-dazhi-maminikweyang." "Ahaw goda," gaa-izhi-ipizoyaang imaa.

[3] Aaniish-naa megwaa namadabiyaang, gaa-izhi-noondawag awiya, omaa akeyaa ninamanjinikaang namadabi, gaa-izhi-noondawag awiya, dibishkoo go iwidi agaaming ziibiing, madwe-biibaagid. Gegaa go ayaazhikwe enitawag, *"Help!"* enitawag.

[4] "Daga bizindan!" indinaa. "Awiya iwidi agaaming ziibiing ganabaj awiya iwidi gii-pakobiishin. Bizindan." Nashke gewiin bizindang imaa. Mii dash geget, *"Help!"* "*Yeah*, ninoondawaa," ikido. "Besho imaa izhaadaa ziibiing imaa, da-o-bizindawang da-o-nandotawang."

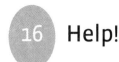 **Help!**

[1] ONE TIME I WAS DRINKING AROUND DOWN IN THE [Twin] Cities when I ran into one of my cousins at the bar. Well, it's getting to be closing time, almost closing time. So we bought some beer to take along with us. Then once the bar closed we headed out.

[2] "Where are we going?" "Oh, over there," he says. "There alongside the Mississippi River. There is a spot there, close to some tables. Right there is where we'll go drink." "Alrighty then," so we pulled up there.

[3] So, while we were sitting there, I heard someone, he's sitting on my left, and I hear someone, like they were across the river, you could hear them hollering. Almost as if they were screaming "Help" is how I heard it, that's what I heard.

[4] "Listen!" I say to him. "There is someone across the river, I think someone fell in over there. Listen." See, he's listening too. And then sure enough, "Help!" "Yeah, I hear him too," he says. "Let's go over there by the river, to go and listen to him, to go and listen for him."

[5] Gaa-izhi-izhaayaang imaa ziibiing. "Bizindan!" "Mii geget, iwidi akeyaa!" "*Yeah*, mii iwidi akeyaa imaa." "Aaniin danaa ge-izhichigeyang da-wiidookawang?" "Nashke, iishpin booziyang iwidi aazhogebizoyang idi chi-aazhoogan, mii iwidi akeyaa." "Aaniin akeyaa da-nagaashkaayangiban, da-bi-mikawang a'aw?" "Aa, namanj naa." Mii geyaabi ko, "*Help!*"

[6] "Aayay, namanj sa naa ge-izhichigewangen?" Gaa-izhi-biimiskotaayaang miinawaa ezhigaabawiyaang, "Aah, daga o-namadabidaa, o-naanaagadawendandaa." Miinawaa oodi, mii miinawaa iwidi niisaajiwan akeyaa, "*Help!*"

[7] "Nashke, mii apii eni-ayaad iwidi. Bizindaw." "*Yeah* geget ninoondawaa." "*Yeah*, nandotawaadaa miinawaa o-bagakitawaadaa." Chi-besho imaa niibawiyaan besho ge niwiijigaabawitawaa. Mii ingwana ojaanzhish, nwaandaagwadinig.

[8] Mii ojaanzhing wenji-gwiishkoshid imaa. Bizindawag, mii ingwana aw gaa-noondamaang. Gaa-izhi-wiindamawag, "Gijaanzhish gosha naa iw gwaashkoshiimagak!" Enh' ginwenzh gaa-paapiyaang imaa.

[5] So we go over to the river. "Listen!" "Yeah, he's over that way!" "Yeah, over that way." "What the heck are we going to do to help him?" "See, if we get in the car and drive over that big bridge over there, that is the way." "Where could we park, to help him?" "Well, I don't know." And still all the while, "Help!"

[6] "Oh no, I don't know what we're going to do." So we turned around again from where we were standing, "Well, how about we go sit down and think about it." Then over there, coming from downstream, "Help!"

[7] "Look, now he is going over there. Listen to him." "Yeah, I hear him." "Let's listen for him again, hear him clearly." So I'm standing real close, real close, and I'm standing with him. It turns out it was his nose, that was what we were hearing.

[8] He was whistling from his nose. As I listened to him, here that was what we heard. So I told him, "That's your ol' nose whistling!" Man, we laughed for a long time out there.

17 Debibizhiweyaang

[1] INGII-PI-WIIJIGIMAA AW NISAYENH *JUNIOR.* NAWAJ IGO ingii-kagiibaadenimaa, mii dash nawaj wiin akina gegoo gii-nitaawichige, gii-inwaazo. Gii-gikendamookaazo. Ingii-kosaa go bangii, ingii-naniizaanenimaa.

[2] Jiigi-zaaga'igan ko imaa ingii-tazhi-nitaawigimin. Aanawi go ogii-nitaawitoon iw jiimaanens. Naa go gaye niin ingii-nitaawitoon. Nawaj igo azhigwa gaa-maajii-maminikwed, mii ko gii-baamishkaad iwidi.

[3] Azhigwa dash igo gaa-ani-akiwenziiyensiwiyaang, apane imaa Chi-ziibing imaa *St. Croix River,* mii iwidi ko gii-poozitoowaad iniw jiimaanan miish iw Chi-ziibi gii-pimishkaawaad chi-waasa ko gii-izhaawag gii-tazhi-agwaataawaad, akina awiya.

[4] Miish ingii-waanda-aanoozomig apane, "Indaga jiimaaning bi-wiijiiwishin ingoding." Aaniish-naa ingii-naniizaanenimaa, nawaj igo gii-kagiibaadizi a'aw akiwenzhiiyish. Gaa-izhi-nakomag aabiding, "Ahaw goda ga-boozimin." Aaniish-naa, ingii-nitaawitoon iw jiimaan. Gaa wiikaa ingii-konabishkaasiin niin.

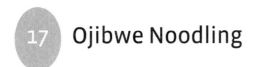

17 Ojibwe Noodling

[1] I GREW UP WITH MY OLDER BROTHER, JUNIOR. I THOUGHT he was rather foolish, he was better at everything, according to him at least. He pretended to know everything. I was leery of him a little bit; I thought he was dangerous.

[2] We grew up by the lake. He did know a little about canoeing. And I did as well. Eventually, as he started drinking a little bit, he used to go paddling around.

[3] As we started to become old men, they would always load their canoes on the St. Croix River and then they would paddle a long ways down to where they would end their trek, everybody did it.

[4] He was always bugging me to go, "Come with me in the canoe sometime." I was still leery of him, that old man was still foolish. So I agreed with him one time, "Okay then, let's get in the boat." After all, I am skilled with a canoe. I never tipped over in a boat, not me.

[5] Miish azhigwa omaa wii-pooziyaang imaa
jiimaaning, aaniish-naa baataniinowag omaa
indinawemaaganinaanig gaye waa-wiijiiwiyangidwaa.
Gaa-izhi-booziyaang idi jiimaaning idi niigaan wii-
onabiyaan azhigwa, bizaanabiyaan nibaabii'aa imaa
da-boozid gaye wiin. Aah anooj imaa baa-izhichige,
boozitood akina gegoo. Gegaa ko ingonabishkaag.

[6] Miish azhigwa gaa-izhi-boozid azhigwa wii-
namadabid gaa-izhi-bishagwaakwiid. Mii imaa gaa-izhi-
gonabishkawid a'aw akiwenzhiiyish, baapi'igooyaang
imaa, gii-konabishkaayaang.

[7] Geget gagiibaadizi a'aw akiwenzhiiyish.
"Aaniin ezhichigeyeg?" ikidowag ingiw. "Aa,
ninoojigiigoonyiwemin omaa, anishaa *noodling*
indizhichigemin."

[5] So now we're getting into the boat, and we had all kinds of relatives there too, that were going to go along with us. So I got into the boat, toward the front, and I'm getting ready to sit down, I was sitting still, waiting for him to get in. Oh, he was going around doing all kinds of things, loading up everything. He almost tipped me over more than once.

[6] Then when he got into the boat to sit down, he missed what he was grabbing onto. Then that old man flipped us over in the boat, jeez they laughed at us. So there we were tipped over.

[7] Yes, that old man is foolish. "What are you guys doing?" they said. "Ah, we're just fishing, we're just noodling here for the heck of it."

18 Chi-maminikweyaang

[1] AABIDING INGOJI INGII-ASHI-NIIZHWAASO-BIBOONAGIZIMIN maagizhaa ashi-ishwaaso-biboonagiziwaangen mii dash aw *Junior* gaa-paa-wiijiiwag ingii-adaawe odaabaan. Mii dash gaa-izhi-ishkosed gomaa minik aw zhooniyaa.

[2] Zhigwa ani-onaagoshig, "Aaniish ge-izhichigeyang," indinaa. "Daga zhingobaaboo adaawedaa!" "Ahaw goda." Gaa-izhi-izhaayaang iwidi *Wisconsin*, idi gii-miinigooyaang zhingobaaboo ningodosag. Ganabaj niiwaabik ingii-izhi-diba'aamin ningodosag zhingobaaboo baa-minikweyaang. Gii-piboon gaye gii-gichi-gisinaa.

[3] Aah babaamibizoyaan azhigwa go niibaa-dibik, azhigwa inaakizigeyaang. Mii gaa-izhi-ishkwaa-anokiimagak iw ebizigemagak. Mii azhigwa giikajiyaang babaamibizoyaang imaa. "Aaniin danaa ge-izhichigeyang?" ingawajimin gaye, booch igo gaye niwii-minikwemin nawaj.

[4] Namanj gaa-izhichigewaangen imaa gaa-izhi-baakaakonangid aw odaabaan imaa ishkweyaang gii-atemagad imaa chi-makak. Ani-nandobijigeyaang imaa, mii iniw ikwe-biizikiiganishan imaa gaa-ategin, chi-ikwe-giboodiyegwaazonag miinawaa ikwe-bagiwayaanan.

18 Die-hard Drinkers

[1] ONE TIME WHEN WE WERE ABOUT SEVENTEEN OR MAYBE we must have been eighteen years old, I was traveling around with Junior, I had just bought a car. I had a bunch of money left over.

[2] As it was getting dark, "What are we going to do?" I said to him. "Come on let's go buy some beer!" "Okay, then." So we headed over to Wisconsin, we were given a case of beer. I think we paid four dollars for a case of beer when we were going around drinking. It was winter too, and it was really cold.

[3] We were riding around, and it was getting into the night, we were getting buzzed. So then the heater quit working. Now we were getting cold driving around. "What the heck are we going to do?" We're dang near freezing to death, and of course we wanted to keep drinking.

[4] I don't know what we were doing, but we opened the trunk and there was a big box sitting in there. As we were digging around in there, there were some old women's clothes that were in there, big women's pants and women's blouses.

[5] "Daga biizikandaa onow! Giga-giizhookaagomin
megwaa minikweyang." "Ahaw." Gaa-izhi-
baabiitookonayeyaang iniw ikwe-biizikiiganishan. Mii
go gii-abizoyaang gii-kiizhooziyaang babaamibizoyaang
megwaa biizikamaang iniw ikwe-biizikiiganishan.

[6] Azhigwa dash gaa-kiiwebizoyaang gaa-ishkwaa-
minikweyaang, ingii-kiiwashkwebiimin biindigeyaang
imaa gaa-taayaang, zhigwa wayaabang ingii-noondawaa
aw mindimooyenh gaa-nitaawigi'id, "Aaniin danaa
aapidekamig ezhiwebiziyeg?" "Aaniin dash?" "Ke gosha
ezhinaagoziyeg! Eniwek sa go gegiibaadiziyeg!"

[7] Ganawaabandiyaang imaa geyaabi gaa-izhi-
biizikamaang chi-niibowa iniw ikwe-biizikiiganishan.
Aaniish-naa niwii-minikwemin niwii-kiizhoozimin.

[5] "Let's put these on! These will keep us warm while we drink." "Okay." So we layered ourselves with those old women's clothes. Then we stayed warm riding around while wearing those ol' women's clothes.

[6] After we drove home, when we were finished drinking, we were drunk going into our house, after the sun had come up, I heard that old lady that raised me, "What in the heck is wrong with you guys?" "Why?" "Well, look at how you look! Man, you guys are foolish!"

[7] When we looked at each other, we were still wearing a whole bunch of those old-lady clothes. Well, after all, we wanted to drink, and we wanted to stay warm.

19 Waabooyaanish

[1] MEWINZHA KO GII-NIIMI'IDIWAAD IMAA
niimi'idiiwigamigong, mii imaa agwajiing gaa-
onzaabiyaang. Aaniish-naa ingii-minikwemin gaye.
Wa, ingii-mayaginawaa awiya ikwezens imaa gaa-
piindiged, waanda-jiikinaagozi gaye.

[2] Wa. "Aaniish-naa ge-doodawag aw da-
wiijishimotawag?" indinendam. Mii iw
waawiizhaandiwaad imaa biindig, ikwe-niimi'iding.
Gaa-o-izhi-booziyaan imaa indoodaabaaning imaa
nawaj wii-minikweyaan. Gaa-izhi-maaminonendamaan
apabaadamaan ow waabooyaanish imaa
indoodaabaaning. Gii-waanda-zhoozhawaamagad gaye.

[3] "Oonh! Ganabaj inga-o-wiizhaamaa." Miish iw gaa-
aabajitooyaan iw waabooyaanish imaa epabaadamaan,
baapaawa'amaan imaa agwajiing babiskiiginamaan
da-onaajiwang gaye. Aah imbaabii'aa miinawaa
da-maajii'igaadeg ikwe-nagamon mii iw wii-o-
wiizhaangeyaan.

[4] Zhigwa sa geget maajiwebinigewag miinawaa
ikwe-nagamowaad. Gii-nanaamadabi aw ikwezens,
"Aayahay," wewiib gaa-izhi-biindigeyaan imaa
niimi'idiiwigamigong gii-o-miinag aw ikwezens waanda-
jiikinaagozi gii-o-miinag iw waabooyaan, "Wayaa,"
gagwaanisagibagizo imaa da-bi-wiijishimotawid.

19 That Ol' Blanket

[1] A LONG TIME AGO WHEN THEY USED TO HAVE DANCES at the dance hall, we used to watch from the outside. Of course, we were drinking. *Wa*, I noticed a girl I had never seen before that had gone inside there, and she was cute too.

[2] *Wa*. "What could I do to make her dance with me?" I thought while they were exchanging blankets with each other there inside during the ladies' dance. So I got in my car and drank some more. I then realized I was sitting on an old blanket there inside of my car. It was just filthy too.

[3] "Oh! I think I'll go invite her to dance." That is what I used, that old blanket I was sitting on, I shook it off, folded it up so it would look decent too. Ah, I was waiting for them to start another sidestep to go offer my invitation to dance.

[4] Sure enough they started another sidestep beat and started singing. She was sitting over there, "Here goes nothing!" so I hurried into the dance hall to give that cute girl that blanket, "Wayaa!" she jumped up straight out of her seat just eagerly to come dance with me.

[5] Mii imaa gaa-onji-gikenimag dash. Miinawaa gaa-
ishkwaa-nagamong miinawaa bezhig imaa gii-pi-azhe-
miizhid. Awegodogwen gaa-miizhigwen maagizhaa
bezhigwaabik. Mii gii-wiijishimotawag, mii imaa gaa-
onji-gikenimag dash.

[6] Wayaahay inganawaabamig aw nimaamaayiban
iwidi namadabid idi aasamayi'ii chi-nanishkaabamid
aw mindimooyenh ogii-gikendaan gaa-ondinamaan iw
waabooyaanish. Wewiib gaa-izhi-zaaga'amaan gegoo
dabwaa-izhid. Mii gii-nagadenimag aw ikwezens. Mii iw.

[5] That is how I got to know her. After the song was over, she came and gave me another one back. I don't know what it was that she gave me; maybe it was a dollar. So I danced with her and that is how I started to know her then.

[6] For crying out loud, my mom was watching me from where she was sitting across the room glaring at me because she knew where I had gotten that old blanket. So I exited really quickly before she could say anything to me. I had gotten myself acquainted with that girl. That's it.

Bishaga'aakweyaang
Chi-obizaan

[1] ANOOJ KO INGII-INANOKII IWIDI GAA-TAZHI-
nitaawigiyaan wii-kashki'agwaa ingiw zhooniyaansag.
Shke ingoji go ingii-ashi-naano-biboonagiz ingii-
ayaawaa go gayat gaye odaabaan. Mii dash iw
gii-pishaga'aakweyaan imaa gaawiin awiya ingii-
mikawaasiin ge-wiidookawid. Gaa-izhi-mikwenimag aw
Chi-obizaan iwidi ayayaad idi endaad gaye wiin.

[2] Gaa-o-izhi-gagwejimag, "Daga bi-wiidookawishin
da-bishaga'aakweyang." "Ahaw goda," ikido.
Mii iwidi gaa-izhi-wiindamawag idi waa-tazhi-
bishaga'aakweyaang. Zhigwa wayaabaninig gaye wiin
idi bagamibizo, gaa-noogitaad imaa, gewiin gabaad,
onawapwaan gaye odayaan. Mii omaa besho imaa
gii-izhaayaang jiigikana imaa okwaakoshinoog ingiw
azaadiinsag.

[3] "Mii ingiw ge-dazhiikawangig," indinaa. "Ahaw
goda." Wa. Niwaanda-dadaatabiimin gaye. Zhigwa idi
ninoondawaa idi biijibizod odaabaan biidwewebizod
odaabaan ninoondawaa, "Na, awiya wii-pimibizo!" Mii
go naa gaa-izhi-gichi-maajiibatood iwidi megwayaak gii-
o-gawishimwebagizod.

20 When I Peeled Pulp with Obizaan

[1] I USED TO DO ALL KINDS OF WORK OVER WHERE I WAS raised to earn that money. See, sometime when I was around fifteen years old, I already had a car. And I was going to peel pulp, but I couldn't find anybody to help me. So then I remembered that Obizaan was always over there at his house.

[2] So I went over and asked him, "Come on and help me peel pulp." "Alrighty then," he said. So there is when I told him where we would be peeling pulp. So then in the morning, he came pulling up; he stopped there, he got out of the car and he had his lunch too. We went real close by here along the road; the popples were piled up.

[3] "Those are the ones we'll work on," I said to him. "Okay then." *Wa.* We were just quick too. When he heard a car coming, coming toward us, I heard it, "Somebody's coming by here!" So off he ran into the woods. He went and quickly laid down there.

[4] "Aaniin danaa ezhiwebizid?" indinenimaa.
Zhigwa gaa-pimibizod odaabaan zhigwa miinawaa
biidaasamosed. "Inga-waabamig awiya ezhichigeyaan."
Gaawiin gegoo indinenimaasiin. Miinawaa
maajitaayaang miinawaa mii zhigwa biidwewebizod
bezhig odaabaan miinawaa imaa maajiibatood da-o-
gawishimwebagizod idi megwayaak.

[5] Ganabaj eta go ningo-giizhik ingii-wiidookaag.
Namanj minik gaa-apatoogwen idi megwayaak o-gaazod
aaniish-naa ogii-agadendaan iw da-waabamind iw
bishaga'aakwed gaye wiin. Mii aw Chi-obizaan. "Enh',
indawaaj gaawiin miinawaa indaa-wiidookaagosiin,"
indinenimaa. Meta go ningo-giizhik gii-wiidookawid.

[4] I was thinking, "What the heck is wrong with this guy?" And after the car went by he came walking back. "Somebody will see me doing this." I didn't think anything of it. We got started again, another car came by, and again he took off running to go lay down over in the woods.

[5] I think it was only one day he helped me. I don't know how many times he ran off to hide in the woods, he was ashamed to be seen cutting pulp. That's Chi-obizaan. "Well, I don't think he will be helping me out again," I thought. It was only one day that he helped me.

21 Aamoog

[1] APANE KO GII-PAA-WIIJIIWAG A'AW NIZHISHENYIBAN
Norman Clark, anooj ko ingii-paa-izhichigemin ke anooj
ge ingii-paa-minikwemin, baa-minawaanigoziyaang.
Miinawaa go ge weweni ko ingii-aabaakawizimin
ko aaningodinong gegoo wii-izhichigeyaang.
Azhigwa sa aabiding azhigwa wii-maajitaawaad
wii-manoominikewaad, gaye niinawind gaa-izhi-
ozhiitaayaang wii-manoominikeyaang gaa-naano-
giizhigak. "Mii waabang da-bawa'amang." "Ahaw."

[2] Booch dash akawe gii-naano-giizhigak, booch
dash akawe gii-paa-minikweyaang, bebakaan
ziiginigewigamigoon baa-baabiindigeyaang. Miish
genapii gaa-izhi-giiwashkwebiiyaang dash aayay. Haa,
azhigwa gaa-kibaakwa'igaadeg, "Daga ani-giiwedaa.
Giwii-manoominikemin gosha naa waabang." "Haw,"
ikido. Mii gaa-izhi-azhegiiweyaang gii-o-gawibiiyaang.
Azhigwa dash gigizhebaawagak, "Ambe zhigwa
boozitoodaa jiimaan, akina gegoo waa-aabajitooyang."
"Ahaw," ikido. Gii-izhaayaang iwidi zaaga'iganing waa-
tazhi-bawa'amaang. Inashke ingii-gikendaan igo, gegoo
enaagamijiiyaan imaa nimisadaang. Chi-niibowa dash
i'iw, giziindime'igan gaa-izhi-biindaasowina'amaan,
aaniin ge naa ingoji wii-saaga'amaan.

21 The Bees

[1] I USED TO GO ALL OVER WITH MY UNCLE NORMAN CLARK, going around doing all sorts of things, and we'd drink all over having a great time. We'd come to our senses now and then with what we were doing. Now one time, when they were getting ready for ricing, we too were getting ready to go ricing on Friday. "Tomorrow we will knock rice." "Okay."

[2] We'd absolutely have to, on Fridays; we'd just have to go out drinking, hitting the bars all over. Then, eventually we'd be drunk, oh Christ. Now it's past closing time. "Let's go home. We're going ricing tomorrow." "Okay," he says. So then we went home and passed out. Now in the morning time, "Come on, let's load up the boat with everything we're going to use." "Okay," he says. Then we headed off to the lake where we wanted to knock rice. You see, I just knew I had something brewing in my stomach. But I had loaded up my pockets with a whole bunch of toilet paper, in case I had to use the bathroom somewhere.

[3] Aah mii dash iw azhigwa baa-bawa'amaang imaa.
Nimaanikaag gaye, gaye wiin maanikaago. Niin
dash imbawa'am wiin gaandakii'ige. Mii azhigwa sa
geget azhigwa, ooyaa aapiji niwii-saaga'am. "Wewiib
agwaataadaa imaa, wewiib!" Aaniish-naa ge jiimaanan
baataniinowan imaa be̱baa-bawa'angig baataniinowag.
"Wewiib imaa niwii-agwaataa!" "Aaniin danaa?" "Niwii-
saaga'am. Ganabaj, ganabaj niwii-shaaboowiz." "Haw
goda." Wewiib imaa gaa-izhi-gabaagwaashkwaniyaan
imaa jiimaaning. Noopiming imaa apatooyaan
imaa nendawaabandamaan waa-tazhi-zaaga'amaan.
Mii azhigwa sa geget gaa-ani-naazhwebinag
nigiboodiyegwaazonish, biitooshkiganish. Wa! Mii
azhigwa geget imaa zaaga'amaan, ninoondawaag go
dibishkoo go zagimeg imaa ninoondawaag. Ayeshkam
igo ani-gizhiiwewag, "Aaniin danaa?" Aaniish-naa
megwaa nizhaaboowiz imaa. Wayaa gegwaagindaang
ingiw aamoog owadiswaniwaa imaa ingii-miijidaan.
Mii zhigwa babaa-bakite'owaad imaa akina ingoji ingiw
aamoog, "Oonh yaahay," niwaanda-wiisagaganaamigoog
gaye.

[4] "He!" indinaa. "Boodawen boodawen!" "Aaniin
danaa?" "Nimiijinaag omaa aamoog." Mii zhigwa
baapid, "Wewiib boodawen aamoog nimiijinaag."
Mii imaa akina awiya imaa bebaa-bawa'ang gaa-izhi-
noondawid. Mii ezhi-noondawagwaa baapiwaad iwidi.
"He googiin!" indig. "Googiin!" "Gaawiin. Boodawen!"
Awenesh naa ge-boodawed imaa zaaga'iganing? Aaniish-
naa ingii-nishwanaadendam. Wayaa baapiwaad ingiw
bebaa-bawa'angig imaa akina noondawiwaad imaa.

[3] Okay, now as we are going around knocking rice, I'm hung over, and he is too. I'm knocking and he is poling the boat. You bet the time came, oh jeez, I have to use the bathroom real bad. "Hurry up, let's go to shore, hurry!" Naturally, there are a whole lot of boats out there, and people going about knocking rice. "Hurry up, I want to go to shore!" "What the heck?" "I have to use the bathroom, I think I have the runs." "Alrighty then." So then I jumped out of the boat in a hurry. I took off toward the brush to look for someplace to go to the bathroom. So now I pull down my pants and underwear. Yes! So now I'm really going and I hear something that sounds like mosquitoes. They were gradually getting louder and louder, "What the heck?" After all, I was in the midst of having the runs. Oh jeez, I had crapped on a bees' nest. Now those bees are stinging me all over. "Ah man!" they're really causing me a lot of pain.

[4] "Hey!" I said to him, "Start a fire, start a fire!" "What the heck?" "I'm crapping on bees here." Now he laughs. "Hurry and start a fire, I'm crapping on bees." All of the ricers had heard me. I could hear them laughing at me out there. "Well, dive in to the water!" he says to me. "No, start a fire!" Who the heck would start a fire on the lake? I definitely was out of my wits. Oh jeez, all the ricers were laughing, and they had all heard me out there.

[5] Namanj iidog ge gaa-kiziindime'owaanen, gaawiin ge
ingikendanziin iw chi-apagidamaan iw mazina'iganish
ingoji. Aaniish-naa niwiisagaganaamigoog ingiw
aamoog. Haa gaa-izhi-gaanjwebinamaan iw
jiimaan, "Wewiib! Maada'ookiin idi naawij naawij
iwidi izhaan." Mii gii-pooni'iwaad ingiw aamoog
oonh yaahay niwaanda-wiisagishkaagoog ingiw
niwaanda-wiisagendam gii-pazhiba'owaad imaa gii-
padaka'owaad imaa ingiw aamoog. Wa! Gaawiin ige
imboonaapi'igosiin. Wayaawaabamangidwaa ingiw
Anishinaabeg mii azhigwa ginagaapiwaad igo, "Aaniin
gaa-izhichigeyan idi, Amik?" "Aah ingii-miijinaag
ingiw aamoog." Chi-baapiwaad, "Ingii-noondoon idi
biibaagiyan, gigii-noondaagoo."

[6] Haa booch igo niwii-pawa'am nawaj, niwiisagendam
gaye. Gomaa minik-sh imaa ingii-kashkitoomin
iw manoomin, gomaa minik. "Haa daga mii iw
ningodooshkin ganage go naa gii-pi-de-bawa'amang,
booch adaawaageyang, nawaj ga-minikwemin."
"Ahaw," ikido. Gaa-izhi-agwaataayaang. Mii zhigwa
gii-piinitooyaang iw jiimaan akina manoomin gii-
atooyaang iw imaa mashkimodaang. Geget sa go
ningodooshkin ganage go naa ingii-kashkitoomin.
"Ahaw wewiib giiwedaa, niwii-kiziibiigazhe,
niwiisagaganaamigoog ingiw aamoog." Mii gaawiin
niboonaapi'igosiin. Mii ko ezhi-baashkaapid imaa
ayaapii ko, apaapii.

[5] I don't know whether I wiped or not, I don't know where I threw the ol' toilet paper somewhere. After all, the bees were inflicting me with a great deal of pain. So now we pushed the boat out, "Hurry up! Start poling out to the middle of the lake." Then those bees left me alone, they had put me in some serious pain, I was hurting from those bees stinging and poking me. And he just wouldn't quit laughing at me. Then when we'd see some Shinaabs, they'd chuckle, "What did you do over there, Amik?" "Oh, I crapped on those bees." They'd laugh like hell, "I heard you yelling over there, we heard you."

[6] I just had to knock more rice, and I was in pain too. We were able to get a little bit of rice, a decent amount. "Well, at least we were able to get one bag full of rice, we have to sell it, I want to drink some more." "Okay," he said. Then we made our way back to shore. Now we cleaned out the boat, putting all of the rice into a bag. Yup, we were at least able to get one bag full. "Okay, let's hurry up and get home, I want to take a shower. Those bees really put a hurting on me." He just wouldn't quit laughing at me. He would bust out laughing every now and then, from time to time.

[7] Zhigwa gaa-tagoshinaang idi endaayaang,
oonh yay biindigebatood akina awiya imaa
endaayaang o-wiindamaaged. "He gii-miijinaad iniw
aamoon aw Amik." Wayaa akina awiya baapiwaad
baapi'igooyaan imaa gegaa go ninishkaadiz. Mii
imaa giziibiigazhewigamigong imaa biindigeyaan
imaa zhigwa wii-kiziibiigazheyaan naazhwebinag
ingiboodiyegwaazonish, ashi-niizhwaaswi imaa
ingii-mikawaag ingiw aamoog gii-nibowaad. Namanj
iidog ge gaa-onji-izhiwebiziwaagwen imaa. Miinawaa
ge ingii-paagish, giziibiigazheyaan. Gegaa go ingii-
aakoziishkaagoog ingiw aamoog.

[8] Haa ishkwaa-giziibiigazheyaan gewiin gii-wii-
kiziibiigazhed, "Ahaw goda. O-adaawaagedaa iw
manoomin." Ganabaj ingoji eta ishwaasimidana daso-
dibaabiishkoojigan ingii-kashkitoomin. Aaniish-naa
bezhigwaabik ningo-dibaabiishkoojigan gii-inaginde. Wa.
Mii iw maamiinidiyaang ani-daashkinamaadizoyaang
aw zhooniyaa, niimidana gewiin miinawaa geniin
niimidana. "Ahaw nawaj minikwedaa." "Ahaw goda."

[9] Haa biindigeyaang imaa ziiginigewigamigong wayaa
gii-paapiwaad ingiw Anishinaabeg. Mii go mii go dabwaa-
biindigeyaan imaa wiinitam gii-ni-biindiged akina ge
dibaajimod ge gaa-izhiwebiziyaan imaa. Mii imaa ayi'iing
agaaming ezhinikaadeg 'Danbury.' Mii dash akina
awiya gii-o-wiindamawaad. Azhigwa sa gomaa minik
imaa gaa-minikweyaang, "Daga izhaadaa iwidi Misi-
zaaga'iganing. O-minikwedaa iwidi." "Ahaw," ikido. "Inga-
adaawen omooday ge-ni-minikweyang." "Ahaw." Gii-ni-
maajiibizoyaang, ingoji go ningo-diba'igan awashime
ingii-tazhitaamin gii-izhaayaang iwidi. Gii-ayaamagad
imaa ziiginigewigamigong imaa ishkoniganing bezhig.

[7] When we had arrived over at our house, he ran inside to tell everybody. "Hey, Amik crapped on some bees." Again everyone was laughing, laughing at me there almost making me mad. Into the bathroom I went, now wanting to take a shower, I pulled down my pants and found seventeen bees there that had died. I wondered what had happened to them. I was just swelled up too, when I took a shower. Those bees had almost made me sick.

[8] So after I took a shower, he, too, wanted to take a shower. "Alright, let's go sell the rice." I think we were only able to get about eighty pounds of rice. Well, it was one dollar per pound. *Wa.* We then split the money between the two of us, forty for him and forty for me too. "Alright, let's drink some more." "Alrighty then."

[9] Then when we went into the bar, those Shinaabs were laughing. Before I even got inside he went in first, telling the story of what had happened to me out there. This was across the river in what is called Danbury. Then he goes and tells everybody. So now after we had drank a bit, "Come on, let's go to Mille Lacs. Let's go drink over there." "Okay," he said. "I'll buy a bottle for us to drink along the way." "Okay." So then we took off in the car, it was only a little over an hour we spent on the way over there. There was one bar there on the reservation.

[10] Haa biindigeyaang, mii akina awiya gii-noondang
aabige iwidi gaa-izhiwebiziyaan zhebaa. "Tayaa
wenzaamidoonan," indinaa. Namanj gaa-izhi-
noondamowaagwen iw aabige iwidi Misi-zaaga'iganing
gii-ni-dagoshinaang.

[11] Mii iw bezhig gaa-izhiwebiziyaan gii-minikweyaan.
Anooj igo bakaan indaa-dadibaajim omaa gaa-
izhiwebiziyaan gii-minikweyaan. Maagizhaa ingoding
inga-wiindamoon miinawaa. Meta go minik.

[10] When we went inside, everyone had already heard what had happened to me over there that morning. "Christ, you have a big mouth," I told him. I don't know how the heck they had already heard when we had arrived over at Mille Lacs.

[11] That's one thing that happened to me when I was drinking. I could tell all kinds of stories about what happened to me when I was drinking. Maybe sometime I'll tell you another one. That's enough.

22 Gii-paashkijiisijigeyaan

[1] WII-IZHAAYAAN IWIDI CHI-OODENAANG,
akawe indoodaabaan gaa-izhi-izhiwinag imaa
odaabaanikewigamigong. Ogii-aanjitoonaawaa iw
akawe bimide. Gaa-kiizhi'aawaad, gaa-o-izhi-giziibiiginag
indoodaabaan. Azhigwa sa eni-maajiibizoyaan,
bimibizoyaan, gaa-izhi-baashkijiisijigeyaan. Mii opime-
ayi'ii weweni gaa-izhi-ipizoyaan imaa miikanaang.
Enh' gabaayaan imaa, ge-nandawaabamag awenen
gaa-paashkijiishing nizid. Imaa ishkweyaang
namanjinikaang, mii imaa gii-paashkijiishing.

[2] Mii gaa-izhi-baakaakonamaan imaa ishkweyaang,
ateg iniw aabajichiganan. Gaa-izhi-mamag a'aw
ombaakwa'igan. Mii dash imaa anaamidaabaan gii-
shegonag a'aw ombaakwa'igan, gii-mamooyaan iniw
biiwaabikoon ayaabajichigaadegin. Azhigwa gii-
shegosidooyaan imaa ombaakwa'iganing. Bangii igo
ingii-ombaakwa'waa a'aw odaabaan. Mii miinawaa
bezhig ayaazhoosing biiwaabik gii-aabajitooyaan
gii-keshawa'amaan iniw biimiskoniganan. Gaa-
keshawa'amaan, mii akina gaa-izhi-ombaakwa'wag
weweni. Gaa-ombaakwa'wag, mii dash gii-
pakwajibidooyaan iniw biimiskonigaansan gii-
mamag a'aw ozid gaa-paashkijiishing.

22　When I Had a Blowout

[1] WHEN I WANT TO GO TO THE BIG CITY, I FIRST TAKE MY car to the garage. First of all, they changed the oil. When they have finished, I got a car wash. Then when I started off, driving along, I had a blowout. I carefully pulled over onto the shoulder of the road. I got out of the car to look for which one of the tires blew out. It was there in the rear, driver's side, that had blown out.

[2] I then opened up the trunk, where the tools are kept. I then took out the jack. And underneath the car is where I snugly fit the jack, and I took out the tire iron. Now I fit the iron there in the jack. I jacked up the car a little bit. And then again I used the four-way tire iron to loosen up those lug nuts. After loosening them up, I then carefully jacked the car up all the way. After jacking up the car, I took off the lug nuts and took off the tire that had blown.

[3] Mii dash gii-mikawag a'aw bezhig ozid imaa
ataasowining odaabaaning, gii-piichishimag imaa.
Gaa-piichishimag, miinawaa gii-mamooyaan iniw
biimiskonigaansan gii-atooyaan imaa. Bangii go ingii-
mashkawibidoonan. Bangii gaa-mashkawibidooyaan,
mii miinawaa bangii gaa-izhi-naazhaakwa'wag aw
odaabaan. Bangii gaa-naazhaakwa'wag, mii nawaj
gii-mashkawibidooyaan iniw biimiskonigaansan.
Gaa-mashkawa'amaan, mii dash akina gaa-izhi-
naazhaakwa'wag miinawaa odaabaan. Mii dash owapii
gii-mashkawibidooyaan iniw biimiskonigaansan.

[4] Mii dash miinawaa gaa-izhi-mamag a'aw
ombaakwa'igan, gii-azhe-asag imaa odaabaaning
ataasowining, gii-kaasiininjiiyaan miinawaa gii-pooziyaan
imaa odaabaaning, gii-ni-maajiibizoyaan. Azhigwa
oodenaang gaa-tagoshinaan, odaabaanikewigamigong
imaa ingii-noogishkaa. Gii-mamag a'aw ozid imaa
ishkweyaang odaabaaning gaa-paashkijiishing.

[5] Nanaa'idaabaanikewinini gaa-izhi-wiindamawag,
"Gidaa-bagwa'waa ina indoozidaam?" Mii gii-waabamaad,
gii-nandawaabandang i'iw gaa-onji-baashkijiishing.
"Oonh zaga'igan imaa gigii-pizikaan," ikido. "Inga-
bagwa'waa goda." Mii dash gii-kiichigonang i'iw
wayaawiyeyaag chi-biiwaabik. Mii dash imaa gaa-izhi-
noominang i'iw agokiwasigan, gaa-izhi-atood imaa
bagwa'igan. Agokiwasigan mii iw *cement*. Mii dash
gaa-izhi-atood imaa bagwa'igan. Mii dash neyaab gii-
piichishimaad miinawaa imaa i'iw chi-biiwaabikong
wayaawiyeyaag. Gaa-piichishimaad, mii dash gii-
poodaajii'waad, de-minik igo ogii-poodaajii'waan.
Nisimidana ashi-niswi dibaabiishkoojigan ogii-izhi-
boodaajii'waan.

[3] I then found the spare tire in the trunk of the car and put it on. After putting it on, I took those lug nuts and put them on. I only tightened them a little. After tightening them a bit, I lowered the car a little. After lowering it a little bit, I then tightened the lug nuts some more. After tightening them up, I then let the car down all the way. This is when I fully tightened those lug nuts.

[4] I then took the jack and returned it to its place in the trunk, wiping off my hands and getting back into the car, and motored off again. When arriving in the city, I stopped off at the garage. I took out the tire from the trunk, the one that had blown out.

[5] Then I told that mechanic, "Can you patch my tire?" He looked at it, searching for what had caused the blowout. "Oh, you drove over a nail," he said. "I can patch it." He then took it off of the rim. He then applied the cement, putting it there on the patch. *Agokiwasigan,* that's cement. Then he put it there on the patch. He then put the tire back onto its rim. After putting it on, he then inflated it, the sufficient amount he inflated it to. Thirty-three pounds is how much he inflated it to.

[6] Mii iw dash miinawaa gaa-o-izhi-azhe-asag imaa
odaabaaning ozid. "Aaniish minik?" indinaa a'aw
Chi-mookomaanish. Nisimidana-ashi-naanwaabik
ingii-inagindamaag, gii-pagwa'waad iniw ozidan.
Gaa-izhi-miinag idash i'iw gwayaashkwesing
zhooniyaa-mazina'igan gii-ozhibii'amawag. Shaa go
ingii-kwaashkwesidoon. Gaa wiikaa miinawaa indaa-
waabamaasiin a'aw Chi-mookomaanish. Mii dash iw
gii-pi-maajiibizoyaan. Mii iw.

[6] And then I put my tire back on my car. "How much?" I said to that ol' white guy. He charged me thirty-five dollars to patch my tire. So I gave him a bounced check that I had written for him. For the hell of it I bounced it. I ain't ever going to see that ol' white guy again. I then took back off heading this way. That's it.

23 Ge-dasoozogwen?

[1] MII KO MEWINZHA KO GII-MINIKWEYAANG GII-
kwiiwizensiwiyaang, gii-oshki-ininiiwiyaang baa-
minikweyaang, ingii-nakweshkodaadimin ko dibi igo
imaa jiigikana ko gaa-tazhi-maminikweyaang.

[2] Mii dash ko gaa-izhichigeyaang, iishpin awiya
gidaang odoomoodaam, ozhingobaaboo-makakoons
gidaang ozhingobaaboo, aaniin ezhinikaadeg?
Ozhingobaaboobiiwaabikoonsimiwaan maagizhaa
omoodens iishpin gaa-siikaapidang awiya gaawiin
gegoo gii-ikidosiin, mii imaa gaa-izhi-chi-ombiwebinang
iw odoomoodaam. "Ge-dasoozogwen!" wii-ikido. Wa!
Mii akina nawagikwebagizoyaang imaa, booch awiya
da-dasoozod.

[3] Oonh yay gomaa minik ko gii-tasoozowag. Nashke
niibaa-dibik ingii-tazhitaamin iw, 'Ge-dasoozogwen.'
Aah, waakaagaabawiyaang imaa minikweyaang awiya
ezhi-gidaang odoomoodaam, mii ezhi-ombiwebinang,
"Ge-dasoozogwen!"

[4] Wa. Waninag ko gaa-tasoozojig apaapii.
Aaningodinong ko gaawiin ingii-tasoozosiimin.
Ingii-kiishkindibe'odizomin igo gaye igo. Mii gaa-
izhichigeyaang iwidi Neyaashiing. Dibi igo.

23 Who's Going to Get Hit?

[1] WHEN WE USED TO DRINK WHEN WE WERE YOUNG guys, when we were young men out drinking around, we used to meet up together, anywhere, alongside of the road too, where we would drink.

[2] Then this is what we used to do, if someone drank up their bottle, drank up their beer can or how is it called? His or her beer cans or their bottle, if someone slammed it up, they wouldn't say anything but would throw their bottle way up in the air. "Someone's going to get hit!" they would say. *Wa*, we would all bow our heads real quick because somebody is going to get hit!

[3] Oh, there were several that would get hit. You see, we used to play *ge-dasoozogwen* in the dark. Ah, when we would stand in a circle drinking, someone would finish their bottle, they would throw it up in the air and say, "Who's going to get hit?"

[4] *Wa*. There were plenty of them who got hit from time to time. Sometimes we wouldn't get hit. We used to cut each other's heads too. That's what we did over there at Mille Lacs, or wherever.

Moozoomoo

[1] NASHKE INGII-WAABANDAAN IMAA MAZINA'IGAN
aabiding, noomaya omaa ingii-waabandaan
iw, mazina'igan, iw inaakonigewin, namanj
ezhinikaadegwen, ezhinikaadegwen *a treaty*? Aaniish
ezhinikaadeg iw *treaty*? Inaakonige-mazina'igan?

[2] Mii imaa chi-mewinzha, namanj igo ingoji go
late 1800s gii-ozhitoowaad iniw *treaties*. Nashke
anooj ogii-inaawaan iniw Chi-mookomaanishan.
Mii imaa daataangigwanechigewaad imaa,
"Aaniish ezhinikaazoyan?" iidog gii-inaawag gaa-
waawiindamaagewaad imaa.

[3] Bezhig iidog a'aw gii-kagwejimind, "Aaniin
ezhinikaazoyan?" "Moozoomoo!" gii-ikido. Miish geget
gaa-izhising imaa mazina'iganing, 'Moozoomoo.' Aah,
gaawiin ganabaj awiya gii-izhinikaazosiin iw mewinzha,
anishaa ogii-inaawaan.

[4] 'Moozoomoo.' Miish iw gii-ozhibii'amawaad a'aw,
"Awegonen iw 'moozoomoo'?" "Mii iw *moose dung*." Gii-
izhinikaazo. Ganabaj gaawiin awiya ogii-pawaadanziin
iw moozoomoo.

24 Moose Dung

[1] SO I SAW THIS PAPER ONE TIME, JUST RECENTLY HERE I saw that paper, that legal document, I don't know what the heck you call "a treaty"? What is a treaty called? *Inaakonige-mazina'igan?*

[2] It was a long time ago, I don't know when, sometime around the late 1800s, when they made those treaties. You see, they told the white man all kinds of crazy things. It is when they were signing there, "What is your name?" they must have said to them there, when they were explaining things.

[3] Then one of them must have been asked, "What is your name?" "Moose Dung!" he said. That is really how it appears on the paper, "Moose Dung." Oh, I don't think anyone was called that, long ago; they were just messing with them by saying that.

[4] "Moozoomoo." So that is what he had wrote for him, "What is 'moozoomoo'?" "That's moose dung." It was his name. I don't think anyone had a vision or dreamed about moose dung.

119

25 Bagesaanag Maagizhaa Bagaanag?

[1] GEGET ZANAGAD I'IW MAAJAA'IWENG. NASHKE
indooshki-maajitaa gaye niin wiidookaazoyaan imaa
maajaa'iweng, aanawi go apane nibizindawaa aw Chi-
obizaan. Geget wawiingezi a'aw niitaawis.

[2] Aabiding dash gaa-izhi-goshkomid, "Indaga giin
o-maajaa'iwen iwidi, indoojaanimiz omaa wii-
maajaa'iweyaan wiin omaa akeyaa. Gidaa-izhichige
na?" indig. "*Yeah* geget." Miinawaa ninagazitawaa
ko bizindawag. Gaa-izhi-izhaayaan iwidi gii-o-
maajaa'iweyaan.

[3] Ingii-kwayakochigemin sa go miinawaa ge
imbiindaakoojigemin dabwaa-maajitaayaang.
Agwajiing ishkodeng indasaanaan asemaa geniinawind
da-naadamaagoowiziyaang waa-izhichigeyaang. Mii
dash iw gaa-izhichigeyaan.

[4] Mii dash iw gaa-izhichigeyaan gii-
piindaakoojigeyaan geniin dabwaa-maajitaayaang.
Mii dash igo imaa azhigwa niibawiyaan azhigwa imaa
wii-maajitaayaan. Aaniish-naa ingii-piindaakoonaa
aw ge-gwayakosidamaaged iishpin gegoo imaa
wanigiizhweyaan igo gaye wanichigeyaan imaa.

25 Plums or Nuts?

[1] INDEED, DOING FUNERALS IS HARD. SEE, I'M NEW AT helping out at the funerals, although I really do listen to Lee Staples. My cousin is very thorough.

[2] Once he took me by surprise by saying, "Your turn, you go over there and do a funeral, I'm busy doing a funeral over this way. Can you do it?" he said to me. "Yeah." I'm accustomed to listening to him and familiar with his talk. So I went to do the funeral.

[3] We did everything right and we put out our tobacco before we started. We put our tobacco outside in the fire so that we too could get help in what we were doing. So that's what I did.

[4] That is what I did, by putting tobacco out before we started. Now I'm standing up ready to get started. After all, I had given tobacco to the manidoo to correct me if I say something wrong or make a mistake.

[5] Mii dash azhigwa gii-ni-waawiindamawag a'aw
waa-maajaa'ag ge-ni-izhinang iw miikanens akina
gegoo iniw editegin; iniw ode'iminan, miinan,
miskominan. Azhigwa-sh imaa indani-dagoshin imaa,
wii-wiindamaageyaan wiindamawag da-baashkamaad
iniw, hay', mii gaa-izhi-wanendamaan aaniin
ezhinikaazowaad ingiw 'plums'.

[6] Gaa-izhi-wanenimagwaa. Maagizhaa bagesaanag
maagizhaa bagaanag, ingii-wanendaan sa go.
Namanj gaa-ikidowaanen maagizhaa gaa-
kwayakogiizhwewaanen maagizhaa bagesaanag
ingii-ikid miinawaa ge maagizhaa bagaanag ingii-ikid,
namanj.

[7] Namanj igo, awegodogwen gaa-ashamaawagen
aw gaa-maajaa'ag. Maagizhaa *plums* maagizhaa *nuts*
ingii-ashamaa. Aaniish-naa ingii-piindaakoonaa
ge-gwayakosidamaaged.

[8] Mii eta go minik imaa. Geget zanagad iw
ezhichigeng. Awegodogwen gaa-ashamaawagen aw gaa-
maajaad maagizhaa bagaanan maagizhaa bagesaanan?

[5] So then I started to tell the one I was sending off about the journey and everything he will see on that path: the fruits, the strawberries, blueberries, raspberries. Then I got to the part to tell, to tell him when he bites into, dammit, I had forgotten how to say "plums."

[6] I had forgotten them. Maybe they are *bagesaanag* or *bagaanag*, I forgot. I wonder what I said. I might have said it right, maybe I did say *bagesaanag*, or I might have said *bagaanag*, I don't know.

[7] I wonder what I had fed the one that I sent off. Maybe it was plums, maybe it was nuts I fed him. Well, I did offer tobacco to the one who will straighten it out.

[8] That's all for that one. Indeed it is hard for one to do that. I wonder what it was that I had fed to the one that had departed; maybe it was nuts or maybe it was plums?

TEXTUAL NOTES

1 **Gii-nitaawigiyaan**
  [4] <ingii-ningodwaaso-giiziso-biboonagiz>
      → ingii-ningodwaaso-giiziswagiz
  [7] <endazhi-minjiminind> → endazhi-
      minjiminimind
  [7] <gaa-tazhi-ganawenimind> → gaa-tazhi-
      minjiminigaazonid
  [8] <gii-pagamiwinid > → gii-pagamiwizhid
  [9] <da-ganawenimid> → da-ganawenimiwaad
  [14] <gaa-ishwaaso-biboonagiziwaanen> → deleted
  [16] <ingii-nitaa-ojibwemosiin> → deleted
  [17] <ingii-gikinoo'amaage> → ingii-
      gikinoo'amaagoz
  [24] added mii
  [25] <inga-aabaji'aa> → inga-aabajitoon

2 **Aaniin Bagonez!**
No edits.

3 **Akakojiish**
No edits.

4 **Joonya-ish**
No edits.

5   Gizhaagamide
    No edits.

6   Gookooko'oo
    [1]   <ogii-onaadin odoomoodaam> → gaa-izhi-
          mamood chi-omooday
    [1]   added aw Gizhaagamide

7   Biindaakwaan
    No edits.

8   Aano-gii-pakiteganaamid Indedeyiban
    No edits.

9   Gaazhagenzhish
    [3]   added gii-maajaawag

10 Noodinoban
    [7]   <niin> → niinawind (indoodaabaaninaan)

11 Gaa-shizhookang Akiwenzii
    No edits.

12 Ishpidoondinechigewag
    No edits.

13 Manoomin Naa Ogookomisan
    [4]   added odakiwenziimibaniin
    [6]   <Grantsford> → Grantsburg
    [9]   <gii-tagoshin> → gii-pagamibatoo

14   Baa-gaanjwebinamaan Ninibaagan
    [1]   added Mayaami-ziibiing Cloverdale,
         Minnesota
    [1]   added abiitawind

15   Megwayaak
    [2]   <ezhimanji'od> → enamanji'od
    [7]   <mawadisidaadiwaad> → mawadisidiwaad
    [11] <indoojibwemotawaasiwaawaa> →
         indoojibwemotawaasiwaanaanig

16   Wiidookawishin!
    [3]   <ezhitawag> → enitawag
    [4]   <zhiibiing> → ziibiing
    [6]   added ezhigaabawiyaang

17   Debibizhiweyaang
No edits.

18   Chi-maminikweyaang
No edits.

19   Waabooyaanish
    [2]   <apabiwaadamaan> → apabaadamaan
    [3]   <epabiwaadamaan> → epabaadamaan

20   Bishaga'aakweyaang Chi-Obizaan
No edits.

21   Aamoog
No edits.

22   Gii-paashkijiisijigeyaan
[3]   <biimiskwa'iganan, biimiskwa'igaansan>
removed

23   Ge-dasoozogwen?
[2]   <or>

24   Moozoomoo
[4]   <ogii-pawaajigesiin> → ogii-pawaadanziin

25   Bagesaanag Maagizhaa Bagaanag?
No edits.

GLOSSARY

The glossary presented here mainly follows the conventions set forth by the Ojibwe People's Dictionary (online). The abbreviations employed for the various parts of speech are given here:

adv conj	conjunctive adverb
adv deg	degree adverb
adv dub	dubitative adverb
adv gram	grammatical adverb
adv inter	interrogative adverb
adv loc	locational adverb
adv man	manner adverb
adv neg	negative adverb
adv num	number adverb
adv pred	predicative adverb
adv qnt	quantitative adverb
adv tmp	temporal adverb
conj.	conjunct order
dim.	diminutive
inv.	inverse
na	animate noun
na-v	animate participle
nad	dependent animate noun
name pers	personal name
name place	place name
ni	inanimate noun
ni-v	inanimate participle
nid	dependent inanimate noun

pc asp	aspectual particle
pc disc	discourse particle
pc emph	emphatic particle
pc excl	exclamatory particle
pc interj	interjection particle
pej.	pejorative
pl.	plural
pret.	preterit mode
pron dem	demonstrative pronoun
pron dub	dubitative pronoun
pron indf	indefinite pronoun
pron inter	interrogative pronoun
pron per	personal pronoun
pron psl	pausal pronoun
pron sim	similative pronoun
pv dir	direction preverb, pv2
pv lex	lexical preverb, pv4
pv rel	relative preverb, pv3
pv tns	tense/mode preverb, pv1
qnt num	uninflected number
vai+o	animate intransitive verb with object
vai	animate intransitive verb
vai2	animate transitive verb (class 2, -m endings)
vii	inanimate intransitive verb
voc.	vocative form
vta	animate transitive verb
vti	inanimate transtive verb
vti2	inanimate transitive verb (class 2, -oon endings)
vti3	inanimate transitive verb (class 3, -in endings)
vti4	inanimate transitive verb (class 4, -aan endings)

Other abbreviations

h/	animate object or possessor; him, her, it (animate); his, hers
s/he	animate subject: she, he, it (animate)
h/self	himself or herself

abinoojiinh *na* child

abinoojiins *na* baby, infant; *also* abinoojiinyens

abizo *vai* s/he warms up at a heat source

abiitawind *adv loc* in the next room

abiiwigamig *ni* living room

achigaade *vii* it is put in a certain place (by someone), "they" put it in a certain place

adaawangen *vai+o* s/he borrows it, rents from someone

adaawaagen *vai+o* s/he sells

adaawe *vai+o* s/he buys

adaawetamaw *vta* buy for h/

adaawewigamig *ni* a store, a shop

adaawewinini *na* storekeeper, clerk, trader

adoopowin *ni* table

agadendan *vti* be ashamed of it

agaami-zaaga'igan *adv loc* across the lake

agaaming *adv loc* on the other side of a body of water, across a body of water

agaashiinyi *vai* s/he is small

agaawaa *adv deg* barely, hardly

agindan *vti* read it, count it

agindaaso *vai* s/he reads, counts

agoke *vii* it sticks on, adheres

agokiwasigan *ni* glue, paste, cement

agoode *vii* it hangs

agoodoon *vti2* hang it

agoojige *vai* s/he hangs things, hangs laundry
agwajiing *adv loc* outside, outdoors
agwaataa *vai* s/he gets out of the water
ahaw *pc interj* okay, alrighty; *also* haw
ahaw goda *pc interj* alrighty then
a'aw *pron dem* that, the; *also* aw
ajidamoo *na* red squierrel
ajina *adv tmp* a little while
akakojiish *na* woodchuck
akandoo *vai* s/he lies in wait, posts for game
akawe *adv tmp* first, first of all
akeyaa *adv loc* in the direction of, in that way; *also*
    inagakeyaa, gakeyaa, keyaa
aki *ni* earth, land, ground
akina *adv qnt* all, every
akiwenzii *na* old man
akiwenziiyensiwi *vai* he is a little old man, is somewhat
    of an old man
ako- *pv rel* a certain length, as far as, as long as, since
akoozi *vai* s/he is a certain length, is a certain height
akwaabiigad *vii* it is a certain length, it is a certain height
    (string-like)
akwaandawaazh /akwaandawaaN-/ *vta* climb h/
akwaandawe *vai* s/he climbs
amaji' *vta* wake h/
amajim *vta* rouse h/, wake h/ (by vocal noise)
amajise *vai* s/he wakes up suddenly, comes awake
amazikaw *vta* wake h/ (with foot or body)
amazom *vta* rouse, wake h/ (by vocal noise)
ambe *pc interj* attention!, come on!, let's go!
Amik *name pers* Larry Smallwood
anaamayi'ii *adv loc* under it
anaamidaabaan *adv loc* under the car
animose *vai* s/he walks away

anishaa *adv man* just for fun, just for nothing, without
purpose

Anishinaabe *na* a person, a human, an Indian, a Native, a
Shinaab

anishinaabe-gikinoo'amaadiiwigamig *ni* all-Indian school,
boarding school, residential school

Anishinaabens *na* Native child

anishinaabewi *vai* s/he is an Anishinaabe person

aniibiishibagosh *ni* old, dry leaf [pej.]

anokii *vai* s/he works, is working

anooj *adv qnt* all kinds, various

anookii *vai* s/he is hiring, hires others

anoozh /anooN-/ *vta* hire h/

apabaadan *vti* sit on it

apagidan *vti* throw it

apane *adv tmp* all the time, always, continually

apatoo *vai* s/he runs in a certain way, runs to a certain place

apaapii *adv tmp* every once in a while, every now and then,
from time to time; *also* ayaapii

apii *adv tmp* at the time, then, when

apiichaa *vii* it is a certain distance

apiichibizo *vai* s/he speeds, drives, flies, runs (as a machine)
at a certain speed

apiish *adv gram* as opposed to, compared to

apiitendaagwad *vii* it is important, it is worthy, it is valued
so high

asemaa *na* tobacco

Asiniikaaning *name place* Sandstone, Minnesota

asham *vta* feed h/

ashi /aS-/ *vta* put h/ there

ashi-bezhigo-biboonagizi *vai* s/he is eleven years old

ashi-ishwaaso-biboonagizi *vai* s/he is eighteen years old

ashi-naano-biboonagizi *vai* s/he is fifteen years old

ashi-niswi *adv num* thirteen

ashi-niizh *adv num* twelve

ashi-niizho-biboonagizi *vai* s/he is twelve years old

ashi-niizhwaaso-biboonagizi *vai* s/he is seventeen years old

ashi-niizhwaaswi *adv num* seventeen

ataasowin *ni* storage compartment, trunk

ate *vii* it is put in a certain place, it is (put) there; *also* atemagad

atoon *vti2* put it in a certain place

aw *pron dem* that, the; *see also* a'aw

awas *adv loc* out of the way, on the other side

awashime *adv deg* more, at least

awegodogwen *pron dub* I don't know what, I wonder what

awegonen *pron inter* what; *also* awegonesh

awegwen *pron dub* I don't know who, I wonder who; *also* awegwesh

awenen *pron inter* who; *also* awenesh

awiya *pron indf* somebody, someone, anybody, anyone

ayadaawe *vai* s/he buys and buys

aya'aa *pron psl* I don't remember who, a being, a thing (animate in gender)

ayayaa *vai* s/he spends an extended amount of time there, is there from time to time

ayaa *vai* s/he is there

ayaamagad *vii* it is there

ayaan *vti4* have it, be in possession of it

ayaapii *adv tmp* every once in a while, every now and then, from time to time; *also* apaapii

ayaaw *vta* have h/, be in possession of h/

ayaazhikwe *vai* s/he screams repeatedly

ayaazhoosing *ni-v* four-way tire iron

ayeshkam *adv deg* gradually, little by little, less and less, more and more

ayi'ii *pron psl* I don't remember what, a thing

ayikido *vai* s/he says and says

ayizhichige *vai* s/he does it over and over, from time to time
azaadiins *na* poplar, aspen, popple tree
azhe- *pv lex* go back, return
azhe-ashi /azhe-aS-/ *vta* put h/ back
azhedakokii *vai* s/he steps backward, steps back
azhegaabawi *vai* s/he stands back, backs up
azhegiiwe *vai* s/he returns, goes back
azhegiiwewizh /azhegiiwewiN-/ *vta* bring h/ back
azhegozi *vai* s/he moves back (as in residence)
azhetaa *vai* s/he backs up
azhewizh /azhewiN-/ *vta* bring h/ back, return h/
azhigwa *adv tmp* already, at this time, now, then; *also* zhigwa

aabajichigan *ni* a tool, something used
aabajichigaade *vii* it is used (by someone), "they" use it
aabaji' *vta* use h/
aabajitoon *vti2* use it
aabawaa *vii* it is warm outside, it is mild weather
aabaakawizi *vai* s/he revives, comes to their senses, snaps
    out of it
aabiding *adv tmp* once, one time, at one time
aabige *adv tmp* immediately, already, right away; *also*
    gaabige, baabige
aabita *adv num* half
aadikwe'igan *ni* steering wheel
aah *pc disc* well, so
aakoshkadeshkaw *vta* give h/ a stomachache (something
    consumed) [inv.]
aakozi *vai* s/he is sick, is ill
aakoziishkaw *vta* make h/ sick, ill (something consumed)
    [inv.]
aamoo *na* bee
aanawi *adv man* despite, anyhow, although, but
aandi *adv inter* where? *also* aaniindi, aandish

aanikanootamaw *vta* translate for h/, interpret for h/

aanind *adv qnt* some

aaningodinong *adv tmp* sometimes, occasionally, every now and then

aaniin *adv inter* how, what, why; *also* aaniish

aaniin *pc interj* greetings!, hello!, what's up?

aaniin danaa *adv inter* what the heck? why the heck? how the heck?

aaniish-naa *pc disc* well, after all, you see, obviously, naturally

aanjidaabaane *vai* s/he changes cars, gets a different car

aanjitoon *vti2* change it, make it different

aanoozom *vta* rile h/ up by speech, convince h/, talk h/ into doing something

aapidaakwa' /aapidaakwa'w-/ *vta* lock h/ up for good, give h/ a life sentence

aapidekamig *pc disc* what the heck!, what the hell!, oh for Christ's sake!

aapiji *adv deg* quite, very much so

aasamayi'ii *adv loc* facing something

aatwaakwabi *vai* s/he sits leaning against a tree or wall

aayay *pc interj* oh for heaven's sake, dang! (expression of contempt, disapproval)

aazhogebizo *vai* s/he drives, speeds, flies across

Aazhoomog *name place* Lake Lena, Minnesota

babaamenim *vta* worry about h/, be preoccupied with h/, be concerned with h/

babaamibizo vai s/he drives, speeds around; *also* baamibizo

babiskiiginan *vti* fold it repeatedly

babiinzikawaagan *ni* a coat, jacket

badaka' /badaka'w-/ *vta* prick, stab, poke h/

badakidamaw *vta* set it up for h/

badakide *vii* it stands erect

badakizo *vai* s/he sticks up, stands up, is erected from a surface

bagakitaw *vta* hear h/ clearly

bagamibatoo *vai* s/he arrives running

bagamibide *vii* it arrives speeding, driving, flying

bagamibizo *vai* s/he arrives speeding, driving, flying

bagamiwizh /bagamiwiN-/ *vta* get h/ there

bagaan *na* nut

bagesaan *na* plum

bagidin *vta* allow h/, offer h/, release h/, set h/ down

bagiwayaan *ni* shirt; *also* babagiwayaan

bagonezi *vai* s/he has a hole

bagwa' /bagwa'w-/ *vta* patch h/

bagwa'igan *ni* a patch

bakaakadozo *vai* s/he is skinny, thin, frail

bakaan *adv man* different

bakiteganaam *vta* hit h/, punch h/

bakobiishin *vai* s/he falls into the water

bakwajibidoon *vti* pluck it, remove it

bakwe' /bakwe'w/ *vta* take a piece of h/, take part off of h/

bakwesidoon *vti2* break it off

bakweyaasin *vii* it comes apart in the wind

bakwezhigaans *na* cookie

bami' *vta* adopt h/, support h/

bangan *vii* it is quiet

bangisin *vii* it falls

bangishin *vai* s/he falls

bangii *adv qnt* a little, a little bit, small amount, few

basikawaazh /basikawaaN-/ *vta* kick h/

bawa'am *vai2* s/he knocks rice

bawaajige *vai* s/he dreams, is dreaming

bazigwa'o *vai* s/he takes off into the air

bazigwaa *vii* it is sticky

bazhiba' /bazhiba'w-/ *vta* stab h/, sting h/ (as a bee)

baabii' *vta* keep waiting for h/

baabiindige *vai* s/he goes in and out repeatedly, enters multiple places

baabiitookonaye *vai* s/he dresses in layers

baagishi *vai* s/he is swollen, swells up

baakaakon *vta* open it (something animate solid or of wood)

baakaakonan *vti* open it (something solid or of wood)

baamaa *adv tmp* later, after a while, eventually, until

baamibizo *vai* s/he drives, speeds around; *also* babaamibizo

baamishkaa *vai* s/he paddles about, goes about in a boat; *also* babaamishkaa

baamose *vai* s/he walks around, walks about; *also* babaamose

baapaawa'an *vti* shake it off

baapi *vai* s/he laughs, is laughing

baapi' *vta* laugh at h/

baashkam *vta* bite into h/ and burst h/

baashkaapi *vai* s/he bursts out laughing, cracks up with laughter

baashkijiisijige *vai* s/he has a blowout (tire)

baashkijiishin *vai* it (animate gender as in a tire) explodes, bursts

baashkiz /baashkizw-/ *vta* shoot h/

baashkizigan *ni* a gun

baashkizigaans *ni* a pistol

baataniinowag *vai* they are many, numerous; *also* baatayiinowag

bebakaan *adv man* all different

bebaa-bawa'angig *na-v* ricers [pl.]

bebezhigooganzhiiwigamig *ni* a horse barn

bekaa *adv man* wait!, hold on!, slow down!

bemibideg ishpiming *ni-v* airplane

besho *adv loc* near, nearby, close

bezhig *adv man* one

bezhigo *vai* s/he is one, is single, alone

bezhigwaabik *na* one dollar

biboon *vii* it is winter

bima'adoo *vai* s/he follows a trail along

bimi-ayaa *vai* s/he goes along

bimibatoo *vai* s/he runs along

bimibide *vii* it speeds, drives, flies along

bimibizo *vai* s/he speeds, drives, flies along

bimide *ni* grease, oil

bimishkaa *vai* s/he goes along in a boat

bimose *vai* s/he walks along

bishaga'aakwe *vai* s/he peels pulp; *also* bishagaakwe

bishigwaakwii *vai* s/he loses their grip

bishkonaw *vta* shoot and miss h/

bishkwaabam *vta* not see h/ anymore, lose sight of h/

bitaakoshin *vai* s/he gets in an accident, falls accidentally

bizaan *adv man* quiet, quietly, still, at peace, content,
   without concern

bizaan-ayaa *vai* s/he is quiet, is still, easygoing; *also* bizaani-
   ayaa

bizaanabi *vai* s/he sits quietly

bizikan *vti* run it over

bizindan *vti* listen to it

bizindaw *vta* listen to h/

bizhishig *adv man* nothing but, pure

biibaagi *vai* s/he yells, hollers

biibaagim *vta* yell at h/, holler out to h/

biichishim *vta* put h/ on (as in a tire)

Biidaanimad *name pers* Pete Nickaboine, and Irvin Sutton

biidaasamose *vai* s/he walks toward here

biidwewebizo *vai* s/he is heard speeding, driving, flying here

biigondibeshin *vai* s/he suffers a head injury

biijibizo *vai* s/he speeds, drives, flies this way

biijibii'amaw *vta* write to h/

biimiskonigan *ni* lug nut; *also* biimiskonigaans

biimiskotaa *vai* s/he spins around

biindaakoojige *vai* s/he makes a tobacco offering

biindaakoozh /biindaakooN-/ *vta* make a tobacco offering to h/

biindaakwaan *na* chewing tobacco, snuff

biindaakwe *vai* s/he chews tobacco

biindaasowina'an *vti* put it in pocket

biindig *adv loc* inside, indoors

biindige *vai* s/he enters, goes inside

biindigebatoo *vai* s/he runs inside, runs indoors

biindigeyoode *vai* s/he crawls inside, crawls indoors

biingeyendam *vai2* s/he is perplexed, puzzled

biinish *adv gram* until, up to

biinitoon *vti* clean it

biinjayi'ii *adv loc* inside of it

biinji-jiimaan *adv loc* inside a boat, in the boat

biinjinikeni *vai* s/he sticks their hand arm in

biinjwebin *vta* thrown h/ in

biinjwebinigaazo *vai* s/he is tossed in, thrown in, they throw h/ in

biitookonaye *vai* s/he dresses in layers

biitooshkigan *na* underwear, biitooshkiganish [pej.]

biiwaabik *ni* metal, iron

biizikan *vti* wear it, put it on

biizikaw *vta* wear h/, put h/ on

biizh /biiN-/ *vta* bring h/

booch *adv man* it is certain, it is necessary, no matter what

boodawe *vai* s/he starts a fire

boodaajii' /boodaajii'w-/ *vta* inflate h/ (as in a tire)

boonaapi' *vta* quit laughing at h/

booni' *vta* leave h/ alone

boozi *vai* s/he gets in or on (a vehicle or boat)

boozitoon *vti2* put it in the vehicle, load it into a vehicle

bwaanawi' *vta* be unable to get h/ to do it, unable to manage h/

chi-agaaming *adv loc* across the lake, overseas

chi-aya'aa *na* elder; *also* gichi-aya'aa

chi-aya'aawi *vai* s/he is an elder, is elderly

chi-aazhoogan *ni* a big bridge

chi-besho *adv loc* very close

chi-enigok *adv deg* with great effort, harder!

chi-ganawaabam *vta* glare at h/

chi-gibaakwa'odiwigamig *ni* a prison

chi-gigizheb *adv tmp* very early in the morning

chi-ikwe-giboodiyegwaazon *na* big women's pants

chi-ishpiming *adv loc* way up high, way up above, way up high in the sky

chi-mewinzha *adv tmp* a very long time ago

chi-miikana *ni* a freeway, interstate

Chi-mookomaan *na* white person, American, Chi-mookomaanish [pej.]

Chi-mookomaanens *na* white kid, American kid

Chi-mookomaanikwe *na* white women, American woman

chi-niibowa *adv qnt* a whole lot, very many

Chi-obizaan *name pers* Lee Staples

Chi-oodenaang *name place* Twin Cities

chi-washkamo *vii* it is a sharp curve in the road, chi-washkamog [conj.]

chi-waasa *adv loc* very far

chi-zaaga'igan *ni* a big lake

Chi-ziibing *name place* St. Croix River

da- *pv tns* to, in order to, so that . . . ; *also* ji-

dabwaa- *pv1* before; *also* jibwaa-

daching *adv tmp* certain number of times; *also* dasing

dadaatabii *vai* s/he is quick

dadibaajimo *vai* s/he tells stories, reports

daga *pc disc* come on! please

dagoshin *vai* s/he arrives

dakokaadan *vti* step on it

dakon *vta* hold h/, arrest h/

dakonan *vti* hold it

dakonigozi *vai* s/he is arrested

dakoniwewinini *na* police officer

dakwam *vta* bite h/

danashkadizo *vai* s/he defecates in a certain place

danaapi' *vta* laugh at h/ in a certain place

danaapi'idizo *vai* s/he laughs at self in a certain place

daso-dibaabiishkoojigan *qnt num* certain number of pounds,
    so many pounds

dasoozo *vai* s/he gets trapped, pinned, hit from above

dash *adv conj* but, then, and then, and

dazhi- *pv rel* in a certain place

dazhim *vta* talk about h/, gossip about h/

dazhitaa *vai* s/he plays in a certain place, spends time in a
    certain place

dazhiikaw *vta* work on h/

daa *vai* live, dwell in a certain place

daa- *pv tns* would, could, should

daanginan *vti* touch it

daashkinamaadizo *vai* s/he splits it up for themselves,
    divvies it up for self

daataangigwanechige *vai* s/he signs things

de- *pv lex* enough, a sufficient amount, suitable

de-minik *adv qnt* enough

debibidoon *vti2* catch it, reach it, get hands on it

debibizh /debibiN-/ *vta* catch h/, reach h/, get hands on h/

debibizhiwe *vai* s/he reaches and grabs others, arrests
    others, noodles for fish

debwetaw *vta* believe h/

debweyendan *vti* believe it, believe in it

dedebagonde *vii* it floats in the distance

dewe'igan *na* drum

diba'an *vti* pay for it, measure it

dibaabiishkoojigan *qnt num* pound

dibaajimo *vai* s/he tells a story

dibaajimotaw *vta* tell h/ a story

dibi *adv dub* where, I wonder where

dibikad *vii* it is night

dibikaabaminaagwad *vii* it is pitch-black night

dibishkoo *adv man* just like, for instance, for example, even,
    equal, directly

dinowa *pron sim* certain kind or type of something

doodaw *vta* do something to h/

ebizigemagak *ni-v* a heater

editegin *ni-v* fruits [pl.]

egaashiinyijig *na-v* little ones [pl.]

eko- *pv rel* since, a certain length, as long as (ako- *under IC*)

eko-naaning *adv loc* fifth

Ekobiising *name place* Duxbury, Minnesota

endaso-anama'e-giizhik *adv tmp* every week

endazhi- *pv rel* in a certain place, of a certain place, there
    (dazhi *under IC*)

endazhi-midewing *ni-v* Mide ceremonial grounds

endaad *na-v* h/ home

endaajig *ni-v* the ones who live there, residents [pl.]

endaawaad *ni-v* their home

endaayaang *ni-v* our (excl.) home

enh' *pc disc* yes

enigok *adv man* with effort, harder!

eniwek *adv deg* somewhat, so-so, middling

eshkam *adv deg* gradually

eta *adv deg* only

ezhi- *pv rel* in a certain way, in a certain place, so, there, thus (izhi- *under IC*)

ga- *pv tns* future tense

gabaa *vai* s/he gets off, out (of a boat or vehicle), disembarks

gabaagwaashkwani *vai* s/he jumps off, out (of a boat or vehicle)

gabe-biboon *adv tmp* all winter

gabe-dibik *adv tmp* all night

gabe-giizhik *adv tmp* all day

gaganawaabandan *vti* look at it over and over again

gaganoonidizo *vai* s/he talks to h/self

gaganoozh /gaganooN-/ *vta* talk to h/

gaginagaapi *vai* s/he giggles and giggles

gagiibadiziinsiwi *vai* s/he is a little bit foolish, is a little bit naughty, is a little bit silly

gagiibaadenim *vta* think h/ foolish

gagiibaadizi *vai* s/he is foolish, is naughty, is silly

gagwaanisagibagizo *vai* s/he leaps up in a hurry, moves frantically

gagwe-aada' /gagwe-aada'w/ *vta* try to defeat h/

gagwedwe *vai* s/he asks

gagwejibizo *vai* s/he practices driving

gagwejidaabii'iwe *vai* s/he practices driving

gagwejim *vta* ask h/

ganabaj *adv man* I think so, maybe, perhaps

ganage *adv man* in the least, by any means

ganawaabam *vta* watch h/, look at h/

ganawaabandan *vti* watch it, look at it

ganawaabandiwag *vai* they watch each other, they look at each other [pl.]

ganawendamaage *vai* s/he takes care of it on behalf of the people

ganawenim *vta* take care of h/

ganoozh /ganooN-/ *vta* call h/

gashkaabika'igaazo *vai* s/he is locked up, incarcerated

gashki' *vta* earn h/, prevail over h/, manage h/

gashkitoon *vti2* be able to do it

gawaji *vai* s/he freezes to death

gawaakose *vii* it collapses

gawibii *vai* s/he passes out (from drinking)

gawiskwagizi *vai* s/he bleeds profusely

gawishimo *vai* s/he goes to bed

gawishimwebagizo *vai* s/he jumps down into a lying
    position

gayat *adv tmp* formerly, previously, already

gaye *adv conj* as for, also, too, and; *also* ge

gaa *adv neg* no; *also* gaawiin

gaa wiikaa *adv neg* never; *also* gaawiin wiikaa

gaa- *pv tns* past tense (gii- *under IC*)

gaa-nitaawigi'igojig *na-v* the ones who were raised by h/
    them [pl.] 3'>3p

gaa-nitaawigi'ijig *na-v* the ones who raised me [pl.] 3p>1s

Gaa-zhiigwanaabikokaag *name place* Hinckley, Minnesota

gaagiigido *vai* s/he speaks

gaandakii'ige *vai* s/he poles a boat

gaanjida' /gaanjida'w/ *vta* push h/ using something

gaanjida'an *vti* push it using something

gaanjwebinan *vti* push it

gaasiininjii *vai* s/he wipes hands off

gaawiin *adv neg* no; *also* gaa

gaazo *vai* s/he hides

gaazhagens *na* a cat

ge *adv conj* as for, also, too, and; *also* gaye

ge- *pv tns* future tense in changed conjunct verbs

Gechiwab *name pers* William Premo Sr.

gegaa *adv deg* nearly, almost

geget *adv man* sure, certainly, really, indeed

gego *adv neg* don't

gego ganage *adv neg* don't you dare, don't even!

gegoo *pron indf* something, anything

gegwaagindaang *pc disc* to one's displeasure, surprisingly unpleasing

genapii *adv tmp* after a while, eventually; *also* gegapii

geniin *pron per* I too, me too

geniinawind *pron per* us too, we too, we as well

geshawa'an *vti* loosen it

gewiin *pron per* h/ too; *also* h/

geyaabi *adv tmp* still, yet

gezikwendan *vti* barely remember it, vaguely remember it

gezikwenim *vta* barely remember h/, vaguely remember h/

gibaakwa' /gibaakwa'w-/ *vta* jail h/, imprison h/

gibaakwa'igaade *vii* it is shut, blocked, plugged, dammed (by someone), "they" shut, block, plug, dam it

gibishkaw *vta* block h/

giboodiyegwaazon *na* pants

gichi-babiinzikawaagan *ni* a large coat, parka

gidaan *vti4* eat it up, eat it all

gidimaagizi *vai* s/he is poor, is pitiful, is raggedy

gigizheb *adv tmp* in the morning

gigizhebaawagad *vii* it is morning

gijaanzh *nid* your nose

gijigwaashkwani *vai* s/he jumps off

gikendam *vai2* s/he knows

gikendamookaazo *vai* s/he pretends to know, is a know-it-all

gikendan *vti* know it

gikenim *vta* know h/

gikinoo'amaw *vta* teach h/

gikinoo'amaagekwe *na* a teacher (female)

gikinoo'amaagozi *vai* s/he is a student, goes to school, is taught

gimiskwiim *ni* your blood

gimoodin *vai+o* s/he steals, s/he steals it

ginagaapi *vai* s/he chuckles, giggles

ginoozi *vai* s/he is tall, is long

ginwenzh *adv tmp* for a long time

gisinaa *vii* it is cold outside; *also* gisinaamagad

gishtigwaan *nid* your head

giziibiiga'ige *vai* s/he washes clothes, does laundry

giziibiigazhewigamig *ni* a washroom

giziibiigin *vta* wash h/

giziindime'igan *ni* toilet paper

giziindime'o *vai* s/he wipes (own) butt

Gizhaagamide *name pers* Netaawaash, John Sam

Gizhe-manidoo *name pers* Jesus Christ

gizhiibizo *vai* s/he drives, speeds, flies fast

gizhiikaa *vai* s/he moves fast

gizhiiwe *vai* s/he speaks or sings loud

giichigonan *vti* remove it, take it off

giikaji *vai* s/he is cold

giikam *vta* bite h/, gnaw on h/

giikanaamozo *vai* s/he is smoked

giikaam *vta* argue with h/, quarrel with h/

giimoodanami'aa *vai* s/he secretly prays like a Christian

giimoojichige *vai* s/he does something secretly

giin *pron per* you

giinawind *pron per* us, we (inclusive)

giishkindibe'odizo *vai* s/he cuts (own) head

giishkiingweshin *vai* s/he gets cut on the face, falls and cuts
     face

giiwanimo *vai* s/he tells lies, is deceitful

giiwashkwebii *vai* s/he is drunk, is intoxicated

giiwashkwebiishkaw *vta* get h/ drunk (by consumption)
     [inv.]

giiwe *vai* s/he goes home

giiwebatoo *vai* s/he runs home

giiwebizo *vai* s/he drives home

giiwenh *pc disc* supposedly, so they say, so the story goes

Giiwitaayaaniimad *name pers* Dennis Smallwood

giiwose *vai* s/he hunts; *also* giiyose

giizhibii *vai* s/he finished drinking

giizhi' *vta* finish h/

giizhishin *vai* s/he gets/lies down into a comfortable
    position

giizhiitaa *vai* s/he is finished, done

giizhookaw *vta* keep h/ warm (as in clothing) [inv.]

giizhoozi *vai* s/he is warm

goda *pc emph* [emphatic word]; *also* gwada

gojichige *vai* s/he tries, practices

gomaa *adv deg* some amount, to a middling degree

gomaapii *adv deg* for some time, some distance

gonabibizo *vai* s/he tips over in an automobile; *also*
    gwanabibizo

gonabishkaw *vta* tip h/ over; *also* gwanabishkaw

gonabishkaa *vai* s/he tips over in a boat or canoe; *also*
    gwanabishkaa

gosha *pc emph* [emphatic particle] *also* sha, gosha naa

goshi /goS-/ *vta* fear h/

goshkom *vta* surprise h/ by speech

goshkozi *vai* s/he wakes up, is awake

gotan *vti* fear it

googii *vai* s/he dives

gookooko'oo *na* an owl

goon *na* snow

gwayakochige *vai* s/he does it correctly

gwayakogiizhwe *vai* s/he speaks correctly

gwayakose *vai* it goes smoothly, straight for h/, things
    straighten out for h/

gwayakosidamaage *vai* s/he corrects the mistakes of others

gwaakwaashkwani *vai* s/he jumps and jumps
gwaashkwesidoon *vti2* bounce it
gwaashkwesin *vii* it bounces
gwiinawaabam *vta* be unable to see h/
gwiishkoshi *vai* s/he whistles
gwiishkoshim *vta* whistle at h/
gwiishkoshiimagad *vii* it whistles
gwiiwizens *na* a boy
gwiiwizensiwi *vai* he is a boy

haw *pc interj* okay, alright; *also* ahaw
hay' *pc excl* darn, dammit
haa *adv disc* well
he *pc excl* hey!
heyaa *pc excl* oh dammit!

idash *adv conj* but, then; *also* dash
idi *adv loc* over there; *also* iwidi, oodi
ige *adv conj* also, too, and; *also* gaye, igaye, ge
igo *pc emph* [emphatic word] *also* go
i'iw *pron dem* that, the; *also* iw
i'iwapii *adv tmp* at that time
ikido *vai* s/he says
iko *pc asp* used to, formerly, previously, some time ago,
    customarily; *also* ko
ikwe *na* a woman
ikwe-bagiwayaan *ni* a blouse
ikwe-biizikiiganish *ni* women's clothing [pej.]
ikwe-nagamon *ni* ladies song, sidestep song
ikwe-niimi'iding *ni-v* ladies dance
ikwezens *na* a girl
imaa *adv loc* there
ina *pc disc* [yes/no question word] *also* na
inagindamaw *vta* charge h/ a certain price

inaginde *vii* it has a certain price, cost
ina'am *vai2* s/he sings a certain song, sings a certain way
inamanji'o *vai* s/he feels a certain way
inanokii *vai* s/he has a certain type of occupation
inashke *pc disc* look!, check this out!, you see!; *also* nashke,
    shke, ke
inaabadad *vii* it is used in a certain way, has a certain use
inaabi *vai* s/he looks a certain direction
inaagamijii *vai* s/he has something happening with the
    liquids in the stomach
inaajimo *vai* s/he tells a certain story, tells a story a certain
    way
inaakizige *vai* s/he is catching a buzz
inaakonige-mazina'igan *ni* a treaty
inaakonigewin *ni* a rule, law
inaanimizi *vai* s/he goes to a certain place in fear, is scared
    in a certain way
inaapine *vai* s/he has a certain type of sickness
indaga *pc disc* please; *also* daga
indawaaj *adv man* consequently, rather, therefore
inday *nad* my pet, my dog, my horse
indedeyiban *nad* my (late) father
indinawemaagan *na* my relative
indoozidaam *na* my tire
inendam *vai2* s/he thinks, considers
inenim *vta* think of h/ in a certain way
ingiw *pron dem* those (animate plural)
ingo-diba'igan *adv qnt* one mile, one hour
ingoding *adv tmp* at one time, someday, sometime, at some
    point
ingoji *adv loc* somewhere
ingozis *nad* my son; *also* ingwis [voc.]
ingwana *pc disc* it turns out that, it was just so, so it was that
ingwis *nad* my son

ini *pron dem* that [animate obviative], those [animate obviative]; *also* iniw

inigaa' *vta* abuse, injure, damage, mistreat h/

inigokwaa *vii* it is a certain size

ininamaw *vta* hand it to h/

inini *na* a man

ininiiwi *vai* he is a man

initaw *vta* hear h/ a certain way

iniw *pron dem* that, those obv.

iniw *pron dem* those inan.

inwaazo *vai* s/he thinks according to h/, to their best interpretation, tries with little effect

inwe *vai* s/he speaks a certain language, makes a certain noise

inwewin *ni* a language

ipizo *vai* s/he drives, speeds, motors to a certain place

ishkode *ni* a fire

ishkodens *ni* a match

ishkodewidaabaan *na* a train

ishkon *vta* hold h/ back, spare h/

ishkonigan *ni* a reservation

ishkose *vai* s/he is left over, remains

ishkwagizi *vai* s/he bleeds; *also* iskwagizi

ishkwaa-anokiimagad *vii* it quits working

ishkwaa-ayaa *vai* s/he dies

ishkwaa-gikinoo'amaading *adv tmp* after school

ishkwaa-niibin *vii* it is the end of summer

ishkwaandem *ni* a door

ishkweyaang *adv loc* in the back, behind, in the past

ishpagoozi *vai* s/he sits high up

ishpi-dibik *adv tmp* late at night

ishpidoondinechigan *ni* a high heel, stiletto

ishpidoondinechige *vai* s/he wears high-heels, stilettos

ishpiming *adv loc* up high, above

ishpimisagong *adv loc* upstairs
ishwaachiwag *vai* there are eight of them
ishwaasimidana *adv num* eighty
iw *pron dem* that; *also* i'iw
iwidi *adv loc* over there; *also* idi, oodi
izhaa *vai* s/he goes to a certain place
izhi /iN-/ *vta* say to h/
izhi- *pv rel* in a certain way
izhi-wiinzh /izhi-wiiN-/ *vta* name, call h/ a certain way
izhichige *vai* s/he does something
izhigaabawi *vai* s/he stands a certain way
izhinan *vti* see it a certain way
izhinaagozi *vta* s/he has a certain appearance
izhinikaadan *vti* call it by a certain name
izhinikaade *vii* it is called in a certain way
izhinikaazo *vai* s/he is called a certain way
izhininjiini *vai* s/he moves hand a certain way
izhinizha'amaw *vta* send it to h/
izhinoo' /izhinoo'w-/ *vta* point at h/
izhinoo'an *vti* point at it
izhinoo'ige *vai* s/he points
izhisin *vii* it lies a certain way, it goes a certain way, it is
    written a certain way
izhitwaa *vai* s/he has a certain culture, way of life,
    spirituality
izhiwebad *vii* it happens (an event)
izhiwebizi *vai* s/he has something wrong with them,
    something happen to them, behaves in a certain manner
izhiwizh /izhiwiN-/ *vta* take h/ to a certain place

iidog *pc asp* maybe, must be
iishpin *adv gram* if; *also* giishpin

jaagizan *vti* burn it
jaagizo *vai* s/he burns

jiibaakwewigamig *ni* kitchen

jiigayi'ii *adv loc* alongside of it, along the edge of it

jiigi-chi-zaaga'iganing *adv loc* on the shore of the big lake

jiigi-oodena *adv loc* on the outskirts of town

jiigi-zaaga'igan *adv loc* along the lakeshore

jiigi-ziibi *adv loc* along the river, riverbank; *also* jiigi-ziibiing

jiigibiig *adv loc* on the shore

jiigikana *adv loc* alongside the road, in the ditch

jiikinaagozi *vai* s/he looks great, has an impressive appearance

jiimaan *ni* a boat, canoe jiimaanens [dim.]

Joonya-ish *name pers* William "Junior" Premo, Jr.

ke *pc disc* look!, check this out!, you see!; *also* inashke, nashke, shke

ko *pc asp* formerly, previously, some time ago, it was the custom to . . . ; *also* iko

madwe- *pv lex* audible, being heard, making noise

madwetoo *vai* s/he is heard doing their business

madwezige *vai* s/he is heard firing a gun

maji-izhinikaazh /maji-izhinikaaN-/ *vta* call h/ by a bad name

maji-izhiwebizi *vai* s/he is evil, no good, behaves badly

makak *ni* a box, container

makizin *ni* shoe

mami /mam-/ *vta* take h/

mamigaazo *vai* s/he is taken away

mamigwam *vta* shake h/ around by mouth

maminigobizh /maminigobiN-/ *vta* shake h/, pull h/ back and forth

maminikwe *vai* s/he drinks and drinks

maminogaamo *vai* s/he has a nice physique, is pleasantly plump

mamiikwaazom *vta* brag about h/, boast about h/

mamiikwaazh /mamiikwaaN-/ *vta* brag, boast about h/

mamoon *vti2* take it
manidoo *na* a spirit
manise *vai* s/he cuts firewood, gathers firewood
manoomin *ni* wild rice
Manoomin *name pers* Irvin Sutton
manoominike *vai* s/he harvests wild rice
mashi *adv tmp* yet
mashkawa'an *vti* tighten it using something
mashkawibidoon *vti2* tighten it by hand
mashkimod *ni* a bag, mashkimodaang in the bag [loc.]
mashkosiw(an) *ni* hay, grass; *also* mashkoshiwish [pej.]
mawadishiwe *vai* s/he visits
mawadisidiwag *vai* they visit one another [pl.]
mawinadwaadan *vti* run at it
mayaginaw *vta* perceive h/ as a stranger, fail to recognize h/
mayaamawi-abinoojiinyiwid *na-v* the youngest child
Mayaami-ziibiing *name place* Cloverdale, Minnesota
mazina'igan(an) *ni* book, paper, mazina'igaans [dim.]
    mazina'iganish [pej.]
mazinaakizo *vai* s/he is pictured, is photographed
mazinaakizon *ni* a picture
mazinaatese *vii* it is a movie
mazinaatesijigan *ni* television
Mazhii'iganing *name place* Garrison, Minnesota
maadaginzo *vai* s/he is starts to be counted, is the first of the
    month
maada'ookii *vai* s/he starts poling a boat
maagizhaa *adv man* maybe, perhaps, or; *also* maazhaa
maajaa *vai* s/he leaves, departs
maajaa' *vta* send h/ off, conduct h/ funeral
maajaa'iwe *vai* s/he officiates funerals
maajitaa *vai* s/he starts, begins (an activity)
maajiwebinige *vai* s/he starts the drumbeat
maajiibatoo *vai* s/he starts running, runs off

maajiibizo *vai* s/he starts off in a vehicle, hits the road, speeds off

maajiidoon *vti2* take it along

maajii'igaade *vii* it is started (as in a song), "they" start it

maajiizh /maajiiN-/ *vta* take h/ away

maakinaw *vta* shoot and wound h/

maaminonendam *vai2* s/he realizes, notices something

maaminonendan *vti* realize it

maamiinidiwag *vai* they give to each other [pl.]

maanaadizi *vai* s/he is homely, ugly

maanikaago *vai* s/he is hungover, has a hangover

maanoo *adv man* never mind, let it be, no big deal

maazhaa *adv man* maybe, perhaps, or; *also* maagizhaa

megwayaak *adv loc* in the woods

megwaa *adv tmp* during, while

megwekob *adv loc* in the bush, in the brush

mekadekonayed *na-v* priest

meno-bimaadizid *na-v* the great one

menwaagamig *ni-v* Kool-Aid, juice

meta *adv deg* it is only . . . ; *also* mii eta

mewinzha *adv tmp* a long time ago, long ago, back in the day

mezinaateseg *ni-v* a movie

michi-ozhi' *vta* make h/ by hand

michisagokaade *vii* it is a floor of a boat

midaaso-biboonagizi *vai* s/he is ten years old

midaaso-diba'iganed *vii* it is ten o'clock

midaasozid *qnt num* ten feet

mide-nagamon *ni* mide song

migi *vai* s/he barks

mikaw *vta* find h/

mikigaade *vii* it is found, "they" find it

mikigaazo *vai* s/he is found, "they" find h/

mikodaadizo *vai* s/he finds themselves, discovers who they are mikwanokii *vai* s/he finds work

mikwendam *vai2* s/he remembers, recalls

mikwendan *vti* remember it, recall it

mikwenim *vta* remember h/, recall h/

mina' *vta* give h/ a drink

minawaanigozi *vai* s/he has a good time, has fun, is joyous

mindimooyenh *na* old lady

minik *adv qnt* a certain amount, a certain number, so much, so many

minikwe *vai* s/he drinks

minjimaakwii *vai* s/he clings, holds on to something stick-like (like a railing or a handle)

minjimin *vta* hold h/ in place, keep h/ somewhere

minjiminigaazo *vai* s/he is being held, "they" hold h/

mino-bimaadizi *vai* s/he lives a good life

mino-dakaasin *vii* it cools off nicely

mino-doodaw *vta* be good to h/, be nice to h/, treat h/ well

mino-wiiji'idiwag *vai* they are good together, treat each other well [pl.]

minwendam *vai2* s/he is happy

minwendan *vti* like it

misajidamoo *na* gray squirrel, misajidamoowish [pej.]

Misi-zaaga'iganing *name place* Mille Lacs Lake, Mille Lacs Reservation

Miskobineshiinh *name pers* J. P. Smallwood

miskomin *na* raspberry

miskwii *ni* blood

mitig *na* a tree

mitikamig *adv loc* on the (bare) ground

mizhisha *adv loc* out in the open, in plain sight

mii *adv pred* it is thus that, it is that

mii dash *adv conj* and then; *also* miish

miijidan *vti* crap on it

miijin *vti3* eat it

miijizh /miijiN-/ *vta* crap on h/
miikana *ni* a road, trail
miikonaw *vta* hit h/ dead center, hit h/ right on target
miikwa'an *vti* hit it dead center, nail it, get it just right
miin *ni* a blueberry
miinawaa *adv conj* and, again; *also* naa
miinooj *adv man* nevertheless, reluctantly
miish *adv conj* and then, so then; *also* mii dash
miizii *vai* s/he defacates, takes a crap
miiziiwigamig *ni* a bathroom
miizh /miiN-/ *vta* give it to h/
moo *ni* feces, crap
moonendan *vti* be suspicious of it, suspect it, have a feeling
    about it, sense it
moose *na* a worm
mooshkinebii'an *vti* fill it out (in writing)
moowiwan *vii* it is crappy, it has crap on it
Moozomoo *name pers* Moose Dung

na *pc disc* [yes/no question] *also* ina
na! *pc disc* look!, check this out!, you see!; *also* inashke,
    shke, ke
nabaj *adv man* I think so, maybe, perhaps; *also* ganabaj
nagadenim *vta* be familiar with h/
nagamo *vai* s/he sings, is singing
nagamon *ni* song
nagazitaw *vta* be familiar with the speech of h/, be
    accustomed to h/ sound
nagaashkaa *vai* s/he comes to a stop
nagwaakwii *vai* s/he latches on
na'idaa *adv tmp* coincidentally, it just so happens, just then,
    right at the time
nakodan *vti* answer it, agree to do it
nakom *vta* answer h/

nakweshkaw *vta* meet h/, cross paths with h/
nakweshkodaadiwag *vai* they meet each other [pl.]
nakweyaakwii *vai* s/he catches their grip
namadabi *vai* s/he sits, is sitting
namanj *pron dub* I don't know what, why, I wonder what,
    why
namanjinikaang *adv loc* on the left
nanakweboozi *vai* s/he catches rides
nanaa'idaabaanikewinini *na* a mechanic (male)
nanaakwii *vai* s/he gets ahold of a handle or railing
nanaamadabi *vai* s/he sits around, is sitting around
nandabijigaazo *vai* s/he is searched, "they" search h/
nandawanokii *vai* s/he looks for work
nandawaabam *vta* look for h/
nandawaabandan *vti* look for it
nandobijige *vai* s/he searches for things (with hands)
nandokawechige *vai* s/he looks for tracks, tracks game
nandokawe' *vta* track h/
nandotaw *vta* listen for h/
nandoojiinan *vti* feel for it with the hand
nanishkaabam *vta* look angrily at h/
naniibikim *vta* scold h/
naniizaanenim *vta* think s/he is dangerous
nashke *pc disc* look!, check this out!, you see!; *also* inashke,
    shke, ke, na!
nawagikwebagizo *vai* s/he stands up quickly while bowing
    h/ head
nawaj *adv deg* more
nawapwaan *ni* a packed lunch
nazhikewizi *vai* s/he is alone, single, by themselves
naa *adv conj* and, also, again; *also* miinawaa
naa *pc emph* well
naadamaagoowizi *vai* s/he receives spiritual help
naadin *vti3* go get it, fetch it

naagaj *adv tmp* later
naanaagadawendan *vti* consider it, ponder it
naano-giizhigad *vii* it is Friday
naanoomaya *adv tmp* just recently
naanwaabik *qnt num* five dollars
Naawigiizis *name pers* James Clark
naawij *adv loc* in the middle of the lake
naazh /naaN-/ *vta* go after h/, fetch h/
naazhaakwa' /naazhaakwa'w-/ *vta* lower h/ (as in a car)
naazhwebizh /naazhwebiN-/ *vta* pull h/ down (as in pants)
netamising *adv loc* in the first, first grade
neyaab *adv man* back, return
Neyaashiing *name place* Mille Lacs, District 1, Vineland,
    Minnesota
nibaa *vai* s/he sleeps, is sleeping
nibaagan *ni* a bed
nibewigamig *ni* a bedroom
nibo *vai* s/he dies
nibwaakaa *vai* s/he is smart, is witty
nimaamaa *na* my mother, nimaamaans [dim.]
nimisad *ni* my stomach, nimisadaang [loc.]
ningaabii'an *ni* west, ningaabii'anong [loc.]
ningo-biboon *adv num* one year
ningo-biboonagad *vii* it is one year old
ningo-dibaabiishkoojigan *adv num* one pound
ningo-giizis *adv num* one month
ningo-giizhik *adv num* one day
ningodosag *adv num* one case (of beer)
ningodooshkin *adv num* one bag full
ningodwaak *adv num* one hundred
ningodwaaso-biboonagizi *vai* s/he is six years old
ningodwaaso-giiziswagizi *vai* s/he is six months old
nisayenh *nad* my older brother
nisidawinaw *vta* recognize h/

nisimidana *adv num* thirty

nisimidana-ashi-niizho-biboonagizi *vai* s/he is thirty-two years old

nising *adv tmp* three times, thrice

niso-biboonagizi *vai* s/he is three years old

nisogon *adv num* three days

niswewaan *adv num* three pairs, three sets

nishiime *nad* my younger sibling

nishkaadizi *vai* s/he is angry, is mad

nishtigwaan *nid* my head

nishwanaadendam *vai2* s/he has their thoughts out of sorts

nitam *adv loc* first

nitaa- *pv lex* being good at, being skilled at

nitaawichige *vai* s/he does a good job, is skilled

nitaawigi *vai* s/he grows up

nitaawigi' *vta* raise h/

nitaawitoon *vti2* know how to make, work, operate it

niwiiji'aagan *na* my friend, my playmate

nizid *nid* my foot, my tire

nizhishenh *nad* my maternal uncle, nizhishenyiban *nad-pret*

niibaa-dibik *adv tmp* late at night

niibawi *vai* s/he is standing

niibowa *adv qnt* many, a lot

niigaan *adv loc* ahead, in the front, future

niigaanizi *vai* s/he leads

niijii *nad* my friend

niikimo *vai* s/he growls

niimidana *qnt num* forty

niimi'idiwag *vai* they dance together [pl.]

niimi'idiiwigamig *ni* a dance hall

niin *pron pers* me, I

niinawind *pron pers* us, we (excl.)

niisaajiwan *vii* it flows down, downstream

niisaandawe *vai* s/he climbs down

niisaandawebatoo *vai* s/he runs down
niishtana *qnt num* twenty
niitaawis *nad* my cross-cousin (male-to-male), taawis [voc.]
niiwaabik *qnt num* four dollars
niiwogon *adv num* four days; *also* niiyogon
niizh *adv num* two
niizhing *adv tmp* twice
niizho-biboonagizi *vai* s/he is two years old
niizhwaaso-biboonagizi *vai* s/he is seven years old
niizhwewaan *adv num* two pairs, two sets
Noodinoban *name pers* Joe Shabaiash
noogishkaa *vai* s/he comes to a stop
noogitaa *vai* s/he stops h/ self
noojigiigoonyiwe *vai* s/he is fishing
noomaya *adv tmp* recently, a little while ago
noominan *vti* grease it, oil it, apply it (as a lotion)
noondam *vai2* s/he hears
noondan *vti* hear it
noondaw *vta* hear h/
noondaagwad *vii* it is heard, makes a sound, makes noise
noonde- *pv lex* before the usual time, need to, prematurely
noongom *adv tmp* today, now, nowadays
noopiming *adv loc* in the bush, in the woods (up from the
    water)

o- *pv dir* go to, go over to . . . ; *also* awi-
odaabaan *na* a car
odaabaanikewigamig *ni* a garage
odaabii'iwe *vai* s/he drives
Odaawaa-zaaga'iganing *name place* Lac Courte Oreilles,
    Wisconsin
ode'imin *ni* strawberry
odoodaabaani *vai* s/he has a car
odoomoodaam *ni* h/ bottle

ogichidaawi *vai* s/he is a veteran, warrior, member of the
    military
ogidaakiiwebizo *vai* s/he drives uphill
ogookomisan *nad* h/ grandmother; *also* ookomisan
ogookomisiwaan *nad* their grandmother(s)
ogramaayan *nad* h/ grandmother (slang), ogramaayibaniin
    nad-pret
o'ow *pron dem* this; *also* ow
ojaanimizi *vai* s/he is busy
ojaanzh *nid* h/ nose, ojaanzhish [pej.]
ojibwemo *vai* s/he speaks Ojibwe
ojibwemotaw *vta* speak Ojibwe to h/
Ojibwemowin *ni* Ojibwe language
okwaakoshinoog *vai* they lie in a group [pl.]
okwegan *nid* back of h/ neck, okweganaang [loc.]
omaa *adv loc* here
omaamaayan *na* h/ mother
ombaakwa' /ombaakwa'w-/ *vta* jack h/ up (as in a car)
ombaakwa'igan *na* a jack
ombiwebinan *vti* throw it up high
omooday *ni* a bottle, omoodens [dim.]
onabi *vai* s/he takes a seat, sits down
ona'aangishiiman *nad* h/ in-laws
onaabandan *vti* chose it, select it, pick it out (by sight)
onaagoshin *vii* it is evening, onaagoshig [conj.]
onaajiwan *vii* it is wonderful, beautiful; *also* gonaajiwan,
    gwanaajiwan
onaajiwi *vai* s/he is wonderful, beautiful; *also* gonaajiwi,
    gwanaajiwi
ondamendam *vai2* s/he is worried, preoccupied, in wonder
ondamizi *vai* s/he is busy
ondin *vta* get h/ from a certain place, obtain h/ from a
    certain place
ondinan *vti* get it, obtain it, acquire it from a certain place

ondinige *vai* s/he gets, obtains, acquires things from a
   certain place
onendam *vai2* s/he decides what to do, figures something
   out
ongow *pron dem* these (animate plural)
onizhishin *vii* it is great, nice
oniijaanisan *nad* h/ child, h/ children
onji- *pv rel* for a certain reason, from a certain place, because
onjida *adv man* on purpose, intentionally
onow *pron dem* these (inanimate plural)
onzaabi *vai* s/he looks from a certain place, has a certain
   perspective
onzaam *adv qnt* too much, excessively
onzaamidoon *vai* s/he has a big mouth, talks too much
opikwan *nid* h/ back
opime-ayi'ii *adv loc* off to the side
oshiimeyan *nad* h/ younger sibling(s)
oshki-ininiiwi *vai* he is a young man
oshki-maajitaa *vai* s/he starts over, starts from scratch
oshkinawewi *vai* he is a young man, adolescent boy
ow *pron dem* this (inanimate singular); *also* o'ow
owapii *adv tmp* at this time
owiiji'aaganan *na* h/ friend(s), h/ playmate(s)
owiitaan *nad* h/ brother(s)-in-law; *also* wiitaan
owiitaayi *vai* he has him as a brother-in-law, wewiitaajijig
   na-v
owiiyawen'enyan *nad* h/ namesake(s)
ozid *nid* h/ foot, h/ tire
ozow *nid* h/ tail (of an animal)
ozhibii'amaw *vta* write it for h/
ozhibii'igaade *vii* it is written, "they" write it
ozhibii'igaans *ni* a letter (as in the alphabet)
ozhichigaade *vii* it is made, "they" make it
ozhitoon *vti2* make it

ozhiiginige *vai* s/he rolls a cigarette
ozhiitaa *vai* s/he gets ready, prepares

oodena *ni* a town
oodi *adv loc* over there; *also* iwidi, idi
oonh *pc interj* so, well, oh
ooyaa *pc interj* oh no!

pakite' /bakite'w-/ *vta* hit h/
pegizh *adv pred* I wish, I hope; *also* apegish, ampegish
pwaadii *adv num* forty (loan)

sa *pc disc* [emphatic]
satayaa *pc disc* dang it!, darn it!, oh jeez!

sha *pc emph* [emphatic particle] *also* gosha
shaa *adv man* just for fun, just for nothing, not really,
    without purpose; *also* anishaa
shaangaso-biboonagizi *vai* s/he is nine years old
shke *pc disc* look!, check this out!, you see!; *also* inashke,
    nashke, ke

tayaa *pc disc* [man's expression of mild displeasure or
    disdain]
tayaahay *pc disc* [man's expression of mild displeasure or
    disdain]

wa *pc excl* awesome!, great! excellent!; *also* howa, waah
wadiswan *ni* nest
wa'aw *pron dem* this (animate singular)
wanendam *vai2* s/he forgets
wanendan *vti* forget it
wanenim *vta* forget h/
wanichige *vai* s/he makes a mistake, makes things wrong

wanigiizhwe *vai* s/he makes a mistake speaking,
    mispronounces something
waninag *adv qnt* they are all over, plentiful
wanii'ige *vai* s/he traps
wapii *adv tmp* at that time; *also* apii
wawaaj *adv man* even, despite the unexpected nature of it
wawiingezi *vai* s/he is skillful, does a good job, does
    something well, thorough
wayaa *pc disc* [expression of contempt] *also* wayaahay
wayaahay *pc disc* [expression of contempt] *also* wayaa
wayaawiyeyaag *ni-v* that which is circular
waabam *vta* see h/
waaban *vii* it is tomorrow, it is dawn
waabanda' *vta* show it to h/
waabandan *vti* see it
waabandiwag *vai* they see each other [pl.]
waabang *adv tmp* tomorrow
waabooyaan *ni* a blanket; *also* waabooyaanish [pej.]
waah *pc excl* awesome!, great! excellent!; *also* howa, wa
waakaagaabawi *vai* s/he stands around the outside
    perimeter
waakaa'igan *ni* a house
waasa *adv loc* far away, distant
waasawad *vii* it is far away
Waashtanong *name place* Washington, DC
waawaabam *vta* look h/ over
waawaabandan *vti* look it over
waawaashkeshi *na* a deer
waawiyeyaa *vii* it is a circle, it is circular
waawiijiiw *vta* go with h/ repeatedly
waawiindamaw *vta* explain it to h/
waawiindamaage *vai* s/he explains to people
waawiizhaandiwag *vai* they invite one another to
    participate [pl.]

wegonen *pron inter* what; *see also* awegonen, awegonesh,
    wegonesh
wenesh *pron inter* who; *see also* awenen, awenesh,
    wenesh
wewebanaabii *vai* s/he fishes with a hook and line
weweni *adv man* properly, correctly, respectfully, carefully
wewiib *adv man* hurry!, faster!, in a hurry, quickly
wewiibitaa *vai* s/he hurries (in some work or activity)
wiidabim *vta* sit with h/
wiidigem *vta* marry h/, be married to h/
wiidookaw *vta* help h/
wiidookaazo *vai* s/he helps
wiij'ayaaw *vta* live with h/, stay with h/
wiiji-minikwemaagan *na* drinking partner
wiijigaabawitaw *vta* stand with h/
wiijigim *vta* be raised with h/
wiiji'ayaawidiwag *vai* they live together [pl.]
wiijishimotaw *vta* dance with h/
wiijiiw *vta* go with h/, come with h/, accompany h/
wiikaa *adv tmp* late, ever, seldom
wiikoobizh *vta* pull h/
wiimbizi *vai* s/he is hollow
wiin *pc disc* [contrastive particle]
wiin *pron per* he, she, her, him (third person h/)
wiinawaa *pron per* them, they (third person plural)
wiindamaw *vta* tell h/ about it, inform h/ about it
wiindamaage *vta* s/he tells people about it, informs people
    about it
wiinitam *pron per* h/ first, h/ turn, h/ next
wiisagaganaam *vta* cause h/ pain by hitting
wiisagendam *vai2* s/he is in pain, is hurting, is in mourning
wiisagininjii *vai* s/he has pain in h/ hand, h/ hand hurts
wiisagishkaw *vta* inflict pain on h/ with foot or body
wiisiniwin *ni* prepared food

wiitaan *nad* his brother(s)-in-law; *also* owiitaan
wiitaawaan *nad* their brother(s)-in-law
wiiwakwaan *ni* hat, cap
wiizhaam *vta* invite h/ to participate (such as in dancing)
wiizhaange *vai* s/he invites people to participate (as in
   dancing)

yay *pc interj* oh my, oh my goodness, oh my god
yaahay *pc disc* [expression of contempt] *also* wayaahay

zaga'igan *ni* a nail
zagime *na* mosquito
zaka'an *vti* light it
zanagad *vii* it is difficult, it is hard (to manage)
zayaagakiigin *ni-v* plants [pl.]
zaaga'am *vai2* s/he goes out, goes to the bathroom
zaaga'igan *ni* a lake
zaagewe *vai* s/he comes into view from around a corner
zaagidoode *vai* s/he crawls out
zaagiji-gwaashkwani *vai* s/he jumps out
zaagijibatoo *vai* s/he runs out, goes out running
zaagikwebi *vai* s/he sits with head sticking out
zegizi *vai* s/he is scared
zikowinaagan *ni* spittoon; *also* zikowinaaganish [pej.]
ziibi *ni* river
ziiginigewigamig *ni* tavern, bar
ziigwan *vii* it is spring
ziikaapidan *vti* drink it quickly, slam it up (as in a drink)

zhawabaagii *vai* s/he climbs the tips of flimsy trees
zhawenim *vta* love h/, show compassion to h/, pity h/
zhaaboowizi *vai* s/he has diarrhea; *also* zhaabookaagozi,
   zhaabookawizi
zhaaganaashiimo *vai* s/he speaks English

zhaagwenimo *vai* s/he is a coward, is chicken, is timid, is
    reluctant, lacks confidence, is afraid to do something

zhebaa *adv tmp* this morning (just passed)

zhegon *vta* slide h/ in a tight space, put h/ into a snug space

zhegosidoon *vti2* slide, put it into a tight space

zhegoode *vai* s/he crawls into a tight space

zhigwa *adv tmp* already, now, at this time, then; *also*
    azhigwa

zhingobaaboo *ni* beer

zhingobaaboo-makakoons *ni* beer can

zhingobaaboobiiwaabikoons *ni* beer bottle

zhizhookam *vai2* s/he steps in crap

zhiibaayaa *vii* it has space to go through, there is a passage
    through

zhiibinikeni *vai* s/he extends h/ arms out, raises h/ arm

zhooniyaa *na* money, currency

zhooniyaa-mazina'igan *ni* check

zhooniyaans *na* coin

zhooniyaawigamig *ni* bank

zhoozhawaamagad *vii* it is filthy, it is soiled